Supporting Language & Literacy 3-8

A Practical Guide for Assistants in Classrooms and Nurseries

SECOND EDITION

Suzi Clipson-Boyles

David Fulton Publishers
London

David Fulton Publishers Ltd
Ormond House, 26–27 Boswell Street, London WC1N 3JZ

www.fultonpublishers.co.uk

First published as *Supporting Language and Literacy* in 1996 by David Fulton Publishers. Reprinted 1998 and 1999.

Second edition published 2001

British Library Cataloguing in Publication Data
A catalogue record for this book is available from the British Library

ISBN 1-85346-683-2

The publishers would like to thank Priscilla Sharland for copy-editing and Sophie Cox for proofreading this book.

Typeset by Textype Typesetters, Cambridge
Printed in Great Britain by Bell and Bain Ltd, Glasgow

Contents

Acknowledgements

Many thanks to all the nursery nurses, trainee teachers, teachers, children and parents with whom I have worked over the years and from whom I have learned so much. Thanks also to the children and staff of Dashwood Road County Primary School, Banbury, and Eynsham County Primary School Nursery for allowing their photographs to be included in this book.

Foreword

The transition from home to a more formalised educational group setting takes place at a time when children are already experiencing rapid emotional, intellectual and physical growth. Likewise, the first years in school up to the end of Key Stage 1 need to provide for extensive growth and development, particularly in language and literacy. Opportunities to learn and use communication skills in the early years need to be of the very highest quality for our children.

Research and inspection findings have demonstrated that the quality of such learning relies heavily on the quality of teaching and support from the adults working in those settings. Increasingly, the work of teachers is supported by assisting adults, and where they are well-trained and well-managed such assistants can make a significant impact on children's learning.

This book provides a useful introduction to the centrality of language and literacy to children aged 3–8. Set within the true spirit of partnership, it describes the vital ingredients of reading, writing and oracy and sets them practically within the contexts of curriculum requirements. The book is constructed to enable the reader to reflect usefully on his or her own experience, and additional activities make it an ideal training text for groups. It is a welcome addition to a growing number of high quality materials now available for the current extensive training of teaching assistants and nursery nurses.

Graham Badman
Chief Education Officer
Oxfordshire Education Authority
April 2001

This book is dedicated to my dear friend Gill Barnes to whom I am grateful for many hours of patient support whenever I write books!

Introduction

This book is written with educational settings in mind including Key Stage 1 classes, reception classes, nursery classes and nursery schools. There is no intention to exclude or undervalue the work of other early years settings in which quality learning takes place. Indeed, it is hoped that the book will provide a useful resource for many people who work with young children. However, because of the limited scope of a book this size, it was necessary to write it with a particular focus.

This focus is on adult support for language and literacy learning within the various contexts of educational planning, organisation and provision. Those contexts include the Government's curriculum guidance for the foundation stage, National Curriculum English, the National Literacy Strategy (NLS) and the Additional Literacy Support (ALS). These are introduced in Chapter 2 in preparation for references to them in subsequent chapters. The book considers these within the broader framework of language and literacy learning across the curriculum. Those who work with children need to understand not only *what* those children are learning about language and literacy but also *how* and *when* they are learning.

The quality of children's learning is directly influenced by the quality of support that adults provide. However, such a responsibility requires training, monitoring and feedback. This book aims to offer initial guidance as a starting point for developing knowledge, skills and understanding in this vital area of children's development.

Support staff – a growing work-force

The final decade of the twentieth century marked considerable changes in the roles and responsibilities of those who worked in early years educational settings. A wider range of adults, paid and voluntary, were actively encouraged to become involved in and assist with the work of schools and nurseries, many of them offering help in the classroom on a regular basis. At the same time, there was a gradual introduction of more formal training, for example, the development of National Vocational Qualifications (NVQs) in 1992 started to provide people with opportunities for their work to be monitored, assessed and accredited. This led to a more reflective and developmental approach to vocational training in many areas including early child care and education. The growing recognition that high quality training was an essential element for those who assist with children's learning and development also led to a notable increase in the employment of nursery nurses in infant classrooms and schools. As the name implies, the tendency used to be for nursery nurses to work in nurseries. However, the quality and effectiveness of their training in early years care and education meant that schools also started to recognise their contribution more than ever before by employing them to assist teachers.

Perhaps the most influential change in the para-professional work-force was the commencement, in 1994, of government funding for the training of learning support assistants (LSAs) on Specialist Teacher's Assistant (STA) courses, a further indication of the view that those who work with children need appropriate training if they are to carry out that work more effectively. In 2000, the Government announced a massive recruitment campaign in which 20,000 teaching assistants would be working in schools in England by 2002. This was backed by the publication of high quality induction training materials, greater clarity about roles and responsibilities and smoother provision for assistants to transfer on to teacher training courses.

Such massive changes in the training and status of para-professionals have been accompanied by debates about pay, status and conditions. To discuss these would be beyond the role of this book. Many people now compare teaching with the medical profession, in which teachers and assistants require role-specific training as do doctors, nurses and paramedics. Clearly, supporting the development of children's language and literacy, in whatever capacity, is an enormous responsibility. If we are to ensure the best for our children, it is essential that all adults with whom they learn are working from an informed knowledge base.

Who should use this book?

This book is suitable for private study by individuals who already work with, or are hoping to work with, teachers in early years settings. These might include:

- parents
- foster carers
- volunteer reading organisations
- school governors.

It is also suitable as a core text for those who are currently in training for such roles, for example:

- nursery nurses
- teaching assistants
- NVQ students.

The book can be used by the group leaders who are responsible for such training, for example:

- lecturers in Further Education
- lecturers in Higher Education
- NVQ assessors
- head teachers
- INSET coordinators
- LEA advisers.

Finally, it is hoped that the book will also be useful to:

- teachers

- student teachers
- early years managers

by giving them guidance on how to maximise the effectiveness of those who work under their supervision. The term 'assistant' is used throughout the book to refer to all those who 'assist'. In other words, the term refers to parents, teaching assistants, nursery nurses, volunteer helpers, students and all others who work under the guidance of early years teachers and managers.

How should the book be used?

This book has been written with a particular emphasis on active learning and reflection by the reader. Wherever possible, the theoretical frameworks are illustrated by practical examples of real situations to be found in early years settings. Throughout the chapters there are also activities that relate to what is being discussed. This is to help you link the theory to your own experience, to revise what you have read and to use a range of learning processes to digest it. Some of these activities are supported by photocopiable sheets at the back of the book.

Access to children for the purposes of some of these activities will enhance your learning. Of course this will depend upon whether or not you are currently working in an early years setting. If you do not have current access to children, it is strongly recommended that you arrange visits either through your tutor or independently so that you can develop your learning through direct experiences. Schools are nearly always glad of extra help, so approaching your local head teacher is likely to meet with a warm response, providing you are clear about the purpose of your visits.

Wherever possible, it is important to try and talk to another person about the activities. This will help you to organise your thoughts, evaluate your work and receive some feedback on your progress. Always try to be positive about the feedback. If it is framed as criticism, try to consider how you can use this in a constructive way to learn something new!

Extending your own learning

Clearly, it is impossible to cover every aspect of such a complex subject as language and literacy. The information presented here is only the tip of a very large iceberg! The aim of the book is to stimulate your thinking and awareness, and provide *starting points* for the development of your practice. In order to help you take responsibility for extending your own learning beyond the limits of this book, an additional reading list is included at the end of each chapter.

Note to trainers

The book is designed so that it can be used by groups as well as individuals. At the end of each chapter there are suggestions on how trainers might develop some of the themes in group-work situations, providing additional activities more suited to collaborative learning.

1 Partnerships and teams

This chapter is all about working relationships between assistants and others. It is in two main sections. Firstly, it focuses on the close partnership between teacher and assistant, and secondly it examines the nature of teams. This is designed to help you understand how complex working relationships can be, to reflect upon your own roles within working relationships and your responses to others, and to consider the impact of these dynamics on children's learning.

Partnership in education

In recent years, partnership has become an important theme within education. The 1988 Education Reform Act was particularly influential in encouraging the increased involvement of parents and governors in the work of schools, and changes in the training of teachers have resulted in moves towards increased partnership between schools and training institutions. The term is now applied to many of the working relationships that exist in schools and nurseries, for example parent–teacher, teacher–trainee teacher, teacher–pupil, head teacher–governor and many more. The partnership that is particularly relevant to this book is that between teacher and assistant.

It probably feels, to most assistants, that the working relationships they have with teachers are not 'equal'. After all, the teacher is the manager and, by law, has to take ultimate responsibility for the children in his or her class. However, despite this uneven balance of 'power' the relationship nevertheless requires shared values and common goals which are reached by a clear commitment to working together. Partnership is most effective when both sides understand each other through clear communication, and where decision-making is made through consultation, discussion and honest feedback. Trust and mutual respect are also important elements of partnership, and where all these things are in place a strong and effective bond can be formed. Inevitably, this means higher quality support for children's learning. Let us now consider the contribution that *you* make to your own working partnerships.

When one works closely with another person in the way that teachers and assistants do, it is important to consider the nature of that partnership in order to identify how one's own contribution affects the success of the working relationship. For example, it is sometimes the case that assistants feel reluctant to make suggestions and offer other skills when in fact the teacher would be only too delighted to increase their involvement. By not speaking up, that assistant has deprived the partnership of

---

ACTIVITY 1.1 – Time: 15 minutes

It is always useful for us to reflect regularly on the way we work with others in order to continue developing and improving our working relationships. Think about your current (or most recent) one-to-one working relationship. Write down three strengths and three weaknesses in that partnership. How aware is the other person of the weaknesses? Now make a list of strategies that you might use to tackle the weaknesses. How do you usually deal with problems? Is this effective? Try to discuss your answers with another neutral person.

---

a valuable opportunity for development. In other words, even if you do not feel you have as much decision-making power within your working partnership, you do have an equal responsibility to ensure that the relationship is positive and effective, and the ways in which you relate and respond to your working partner will have a significant impact on the day-to-day quality of your work.

Those who assist in early years settings can have very different experiences of partnership according to the ethos and policies of the workplace, and the working practices of the teachers. Some teachers give their assistants enormous responsibility and opportunities for decision-making whereas others prefer to keep total control of everything.

ACTIVITY 1.2 – Time: 30 minutes

Using Activity Sheet 1 'Reflecting on yourself in working partnerships', consider each question in relation to your current working partnership, or one that you have experienced in the past. Do you feel able to share these thoughts with that partner? If not, ask yourself why, and consider is there anything which you could do to change this?

Partnerships within teams

So far, we have been tending to regard 'partnership' as a two-way relationship, but the meaning of the word has come to mean much more than this. In recent years it has come to represent a particular way of working. In practice, the dynamics of nurseries and schools are complex because they involve groups of people working together rather than simply pairs. When these groups work together in a planned and intentional way they become teams. These teams are therefore mechanisms for partnership.

Teams are interesting! They are composed of mixtures of personalities and roles which lead to a complicated set of interpersonal relationships. In order to develop an awareness of how you work within your team, and why, we will now look more closely at some of the important facts about teams.

The synergy of teams

Imagine eating the ingredients of a Victoria sandwich, but eating them separately – butter, flour, sugar, raw eggs and sweet jam. Then compare this with eating the cake itself – a miraculous transformation of substances into a different and delicious form. Teams are a bit the same. Each individual member has something different to offer and yet the force of the whole team is so much more than merely the sum total of the individual parts. This is known as 'synergy'. Indeed, it can have a power and energy of its own that enhances the quality of the work in a most effective way, which is beneficial to children and adults alike.

There are many types of teams, and those which exist in early years settings are frequently composed of a wide variety of adults: teacher; nursery nurse; paid assistant; unpaid voluntary assistant; parent; governor; student; playgroup leader; and special needs support assistant to name the most obvious. Teams also vary in the way they operate – some show real cohesion and solidarity, whereas others harbour the discomfort of resentment and dissatisfaction.

Early years teams operate at their best where all the members have a commitment to the fact that they are a team and really value working together. They hold a shared vision which springs directly from the needs of the children. Other notable features of effective early years teams are:

- clarity of purpose and direction
- clear understanding of roles and responsibilities
- direct and effective communication
- flexibility and adaptability
- early identification of problems and agreed action for solutions
- clear time plans and deadlines
- well-organised systems
- recognition of the team's strengths and weaknesses
- regular self-assessment of how the team is functioning
- meetings which are effective.

Team meetings

Regular meetings are essential to the effective communication of any team. The five main purposes of meetings are:

1. To plan for future work.
2. To share information.
3. To identify and solve problems.
4. To make decisions.
5. To maintain a sense of group belonging.

The usefulness of such meetings will depend on the team leader to a certain extent, but it is also the responsibility of all team members to ensure that meetings are productive. Teams in which members merely follow their leader's instructions tend to be less productive than those which share and explore ideas with everyone.

ACTIVITY 1.3 – Time: 10 minutes

Pause to think about the following questions. What role do you take in meetings? How do you contribute to the team? How do you feel about the contributions of others?

Team conflict

All teams can expect to experience conflict sometimes. Conflict is inevitable and it is essential that it should be dealt with rather than avoided. However, the way in which teams deal with the conflict can make a significant difference to the outcome and the future health of the team.

It is important to recognise and acknowledge conflict when it arises, to discuss it and try to understand what is really at the root. One way to start is to identify the areas of agreement and disagreement. This is useful to the team because it creates a better understanding, not only of issues but also of each other.

Exploring conflict can be a creative process. Where a satisfactory solution is the outcome, all the team will benefit from a sense of achievement. This will strengthen the team and create healthy growth as opposed to leaving the area of disagreement in a dark corner where it will lurk and fester.

What makes a good team member?

We should not all expect to have the same skills in a team. Just as the cake benefits from different ingredients, so the team benefits from the variety of skills and attitudes that each individual member brings. Nevertheless, it is useful to develop a clear understanding of the general principles that strengthen a team through the quality of the relationships. An ideal team member does not follow unquestioningly, merely performing duties and obeying orders. Such passive behaviour does nothing to help the growth and development of a team and its work. Instead, a team member will contribute constructively and creatively in a variety of ways. These are listed below and have been divided into four main sections.

1. Belief system
A good team member:

-   is committed to the overall success of the team
-   respects the leader but does not expect that leader to take all responsibility
-   has high expectations of the team's work.

2. Self-awareness
A good team member:

-   knows own strengths and skills
-   knows own limitations
-   recognises areas for development in own practice
-   is aware of role within the group
-   knows when to ask for help and advice.

3. Social skills

A good team member:

- supports the needs of others
- is a good listener
- is aware of impact on others
- does not avoid problems
- is committed to exploring conflict and resolving difficulties
- recognises the importance of open and honest relationships
- respects the feelings of others
- respects different viewpoints
- knows when it is appropriate to speak up
- knows when it is more useful to keep quiet

4. Professional skills

A good team member:

- takes advice constructively
- gives advice constructively
- communicates clearly
- works with and not against others
- thinks creatively
- can demonstrate flexibility
- shares the responsibility of decision-making
- is clear about their role but not inflexible
- can work independently without undermining the work of the team
- reflects and builds continuously on own performance and practice.

ACTIVITY 1.4 – Time: 20 minutes and ongoing

Think about the team in which you work. If you are not currently in post think about your training group. Using Activity Sheet 2 'Developing team skills'. Take stock of what you do well, and where you need to develop. Do not overwhelm yourself with too many things all at once. Perhaps take one area of focus each week.

Conclusion

Teams operate effectively where there is a true sense of partnership. Partnership is an ethos, a way of working, a committed relationship between cooperative parties. This way of working involves open dialogue and clarity of purpose shared by all. In early years educational settings the sizes and combinations of teams are varied, but where they work effectively the children benefit from adult support which is built on mutual respect within a cooperative ethos and where the total result is vastly greater than the sum of the parts.

Notes for group leaders

⇨ Discussions about each activity could be carried out in pairs. This would be a safe framework within which to share what may be quite personal thoughts and feelings, rather than opening them up to larger group work. Wherever possible, try to precede this with a general discussion about giving peer support or, for example, how one can best help and encourage ones partner through such discussions.

⇨ Group work is very appropriate for examining team skills. Team building activities in groups of four could include:

- building a structure from newspaper to support a wine bottle
- writing a short story
- planning a hypothetical party
- designing and printing a T-shirt.

⇨ Observing and discussing their roles within the team after the activity is as useful as the team activity itself.

Further reading

DfEE (2000) *Working with Teaching Assistants. A Good Practice Guide.* London: DfEE.

Fox, G. (1998) *A Handbook for Learning Support Assistants.* London: David Fulton Publishers.

Hill, F. and Parsons, L. (1999) *Teamwork in the Management of Emotional and Behavioural Difficulties.* London: David Fulton Publishers.

Mills, J. (1996) *Partnership in the Primary School.* London: Routledge.

Thomas, G. (1992) *Effective Classroom Team-work: Support or Intrusion?* London: Routledge.

2 The centrality of language in early years settings

This chapter begins with brief explanations of the DfEE/QCA's curriculum guidance for the foundation stage (DfEE and QCA 2000), the National Curriculum requirements for English (DfEE and QCA 1999a), the National Literacy Strategy (NLS) (DfEE 1998) and the Additional Literacy Support (ALS) (DfEE 1999). It then goes on to consider the wider implications of language and literacy in the early years including the significance of thought and play. It looks at how adults can support these effectively, and the types of environment that help to stimulate and develop language and literacy.

Since the 1988 Education Reform Act, there have been many government initiatives to help improve the teaching and learning of language and literacy. Even since the first edition of this book, the changes have been considerable, and it is relevant to describe the main ones here. This is intended to help you understand the terminology and background rather than provide full descriptions. However, it is strongly recommended that you look at copies of all the documents relating to the initiatives described in order to understand more of the detail. Publications are listed at the end of the chapter if you wish to order your own copies (some are available free from the DfEE), find them in the library or ask for them in school. Relevant website addresses are also provided.

Curriculum guidance for the foundation stage

Useful guidelines for early years settings receiving nursery grant funding, and schools with nursery and reception aged children, were introduced by the DfEE in 2000 (DfEE and QCA 2000). These are intended to help practitioners plan, assess and teach 3- and 4-year-old children appropriately in order that they can achieve the early learning goals introduced in 1999 (DfEE and QCA 1999b). (The early learning goals are discussed in more detail in Chapter 3.)

The foundation stage curriculum is divided into six areas of learning:

- personal, social and emotional development
- communication, language and literacy
- mathematical development
- knowledge and understanding of the world
- physical development
- creative development.

The second of these is the obvious area of focus for this book, and reference will be made to that section in other chapters. However, it is important to remember that literacy and language are an essential part of everything that young children do, so opportunities for teaching and development in these areas are continuous in early years settings. The guidelines for communication, language and literacy encourage practitioners to provide rich opportunities for speaking and listening, and varied encounters with a wide range of texts (not only stories) within a stimulating environment in which language is recognised as important. One cannot do justice to the full content and value of the foundation curriculum here, but you will find the actual document very user-friendly and full of practical examples.

The National Curriculum requirements for English

Unlike the guidelines just described, the National Curriculum, first introduced in 1988, is a compulsory requirement for state schools. English is one of the three core subjects for the National Curriculum, the other two are maths and science. Welsh replaces English as a core subject in Welsh-speaking schools, where English is not a statutory requirement. In Welsh–English-speaking schools, Welsh is studied as a foundation subject in addition to the English core.

In 1999, a revised version of the National Curriculum was introduced. The Order for English (DfEE and QCA 1999a) contains three Programmes of Study for English: En1, Speaking and Listening; En2, Reading; and En3, Writing. The Orders for English and Welsh stress the interrelatedness of these three modes of language and encourage opportunities for learning in this way by making links between the three sections and across the rest of the curriculum. The Order for English also makes ongoing links with the early learning goals and makes reference to these throughout. Each Programme of Study is divided into two types of requirement. Firstly, knowledge, skills and understanding – what actually has to be taught. Secondly, breadth of study – the contexts within which children will learn (e.g. activities and experiences).

Attainment Targets consisting of Level Descriptions of increasing difficulty set out what children are expected to achieve. At the end of each[1] Key Stage the children are assessed by external tests plus teachers' own assessments known as National Assessment Tasks and Tests (formerly known as Standard Assessment Tests, or 'SATs', a term that many people still use). The average level for a seven-year-old at the end of Key Stage 1 is Level 2, but the full range falls between Levels 1 and 3. The average level for an 11-year-old at the end of Key Stage 2 is Level 4, within the range 2–5.

The National Literacy Strategy (NLS)

The NLS (DfEE 1998) was introduced into schools in England in 1998 as part of the government's drive to raise standards. It is not a statutory requirement but is strongly recommended and the majority of primary schools have now adopted it in one form or another. The NLS provides a framework for teaching consisting of detailed

---

[1]Key Stage 1 = Years 1 and 2; Key Stage 2 = Years 3–6; Key Stage 3 = Years 7–9; Key Stage 4 = Years 10 and 11

objectives for each term (Reception to Year 6) focusing on particular aspects of reading and writing. These are divided into three interrelated 'strands': word level, sentence level and text level. Particular types of texts are specified for each term: fiction, poetry and non-fiction. The strategy also provides a specific approach to literacy instruction which takes place during the daily Literacy Hour combining all the elements of effective teaching and learning such as clear instruction, explanation, demonstration, modelling, questioning, exploring, investigating, discussing, listening and responding. The Literacy Hour begins with whole-class teaching, usually starting with a shared text such as a big book for 15 minutes moving on to word level work for the next 15 minutes. The children then work independently or in ability groups for 20 minutes on a reading or writing task, the teacher working with at least two ability groups each day during this section. During the final 10 minutes the whole class comes together again for a 'pulling together' time in which learning is reviewed and consolidated (e.g. some children may read out what they have written and the teacher reminds the class of the specific teaching points that have been addressed). It is easy to see that assistants can have a valuable part to play in this dynamic and interactive hour of teaching.

The Additional Literacy Support (ALS)

The ALS (DfEE 1999) was introduced one year after the NLS to target children who were falling short of the average for reading and writing, in particular pupils in Years 3 and 4 assessed at Level 2c, and who would normally receive no additional support. The Government produced extensive training materials and some schools received extra funding to recruit and train special learning support assistants (LSAs). The programme is delivered to groups of children for 20 minutes three times a week by an LSA and once by the class teacher (although this is obviously adapted by schools according to available resources). It is made up of four modules each lasting eight weeks, starting with revision and consolidation of Key Stage 1 word level work then moving on to sentence level work, but with a continuous focus on phonics. Every lesson is specified in detail and games and activities can be made from photocopiable sheets provided.

Why is language so important?

The fact that English is at the very core of the National Curriculum is a clear indication of how central our language is to our learning. Not only is it a subject in its own right, it also underpins all other areas of the curriculum. The broad, balanced and holistic curriculum provided in good quality nursery and reception classes will be providing enriching language and literacy activities and opportunities which ensure the continuity of all the developmental processes that have already taken place at home. It is equally important that from the age of five the National Curriculum is delivered through stimulating integrated experiences that are meaningful and enjoyable to children, and which motivate them to engage with learning.

Language is such an integral part of our lives that we often take it for granted. Every day we participate in hundreds of thousands of complex interactions involving people and texts. But have you ever stopped to think what life would be like without language? No talking, no listening to others talking, no print, no books, no media, no vehicle for expressing our feelings and no framework for our thinking. The reality would be that we would feel extremely isolated from each other and all our ways of working and thinking would be altered and significantly reduced.

Language represents the major means of communication between humans and is central to all we do (Figure 2.1). During the first four years of life, a child learns language at a most incredible rate, at a time when she or he is also learning about the world in which she or he lives. If we are to continue nurturing and extending children's language in early years education it is vital that we recognise and value what each child already knows so that we can plan for their continued development.

There have been several different theories about how language is acquired, but the most significant factor that theorists have identified is that *language learning takes place when children are interacting with adults* (Wells 1985.) In everyday life such interactions are numerous and playgroup, nursery or school is only one of the communities within which the child uses language among adults. Figure 2.2 illustrates some of the other contexts in which language is learned and used. Each of these presents the child with a range of different vocabularies, structures and meanings. The situations can also vary enormously in the purposes for which language is used, and most children learn to switch from one to another with remarkable skill.

Figure 2.1 Talk is a vital part of human communication

ACTIVITY 2.1 – Time: 20 minutes

Make a photocopy of Activity Sheet 3 'Variety in language. Choose three of the communities from the selection in Figure 2.2 and record some of the specific features of the language that might take place by thinking about vocabulary and purpose. The purpose can include spoken and written language.

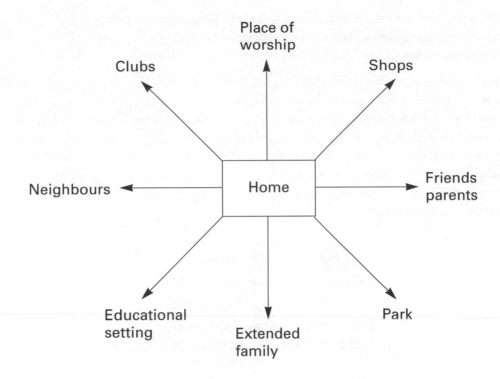

Figure 2.2 Some language communities of the child

Language and learning

Language helps children's learning and learning helps children's language. By the age of four, the complexity and fluency of language acquired represents an amazing achievement, especially when we consider how challenging it is as an adult to learn a new language! If we also consider how many other things a four-year-old knows and understands it becomes clear that a very complex set of processes must be taking place.

To help us identify some of those processes, it is useful to think about the learning of a new language and compare this with the language of the preschool child. In the secondary school situation, even the most dynamic French teacher can only engage in direct exchange with one pupil at a time. The whole class chanting responses in unison is a technique used to increase the number of responses a pupil can make during a lesson, but what is missing from this type of exchange is spontaneity, individual adjustment and fluency of immediate response. A toddler at home with his or her primary carer, on the other hand, is engaging in a continuous stream of conversation, backwards and forwards.

Let us look more closely at what might be assisting that toddler with his or her language development:

- intensive one-to-one interaction
- engaging in a variety of tasks with associated language
- language arising from the child's experiences
- language relating to immediate stimuli

11

- a range of environments and their associated language
- endless supply of visual resources and artefacts
- stories, rhymes and books.

The natural curiosity of young children leads them repeatedly into language learning situations which arise out of normal everyday activities. They are not usually required to wait before they speak as they are in school. Indeed, those who have lived with toddlers will know how continuous and searching their questions can be! The ways in which adults respond to those questions can have a great influence on the development of the child's language. Figure 2.3 illustrates how different responses to the child's questions by the adult can open up or close down the language opportunities for the child.

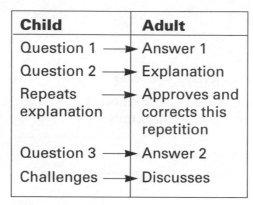

Child	Adult
Question 1 ➤	Answer 1
Question 2 ➤	Explanation
Repeats explanation ➤	Approves and corrects this repetition
Question 3 ➤	Answer 2
Challenges ➤	Discusses

Figure 2.3 Adult engages with the child

In Figure 2.4, however, the adult restricts the flow of subsequent language.

Child	Adult
Question 1 ➤	Answer
Question 2 ➤	Reprimand

Figure 2.4 Adult disengages with the child

When we compare these two simple examples we can see that the adult in Figure 2.3 has opened up a range of opportunities for the child to use language – in this case five separate units. However, in Figure 2.4 those opportunities have been closed down and the child only utters two units in total. If we multiply the number of child units by the number of times in any day when a child initiates talk we can see that the child in the first example is going to have a vastly different experience to the child in the second example. Let us imagine that a child initiates language with an adult approximately 300 times in one day (this is a conservative estimate). The child in Figure 2.3 is likely to have 5×300 opportunities for talking, a total of 1,500 experiences, whereas the child in Figure 2.4 is only likely to have 2×300, a total of 600 experiences. And these calculations are only for one day . . .

Of course, this is a contrived mathematical exercise to illustrate the point and there will always be times when it is not appropriate or convenient to develop the conversation fully. Nevertheless, the example is intended to illustrate how significant the role of the adult is in providing opportunities and enabling experimentation and consolidation of young children's language. Where the language is exchanging backwards and forwards between adult and child, the child is hearing language spoken within a specific context. The child can therefore participate and experiment within that context using the language that is being modelled alongside the language he or she already knows.

As well as the quantity of conversation, it is also necessary to consider the quality of the interchange between child and adult. The child in Figure 2.4 is not only experiencing fewer language opportunities, he or she is also experiencing rejection and lack of respect as a learner. Which child do you think is most likely to feel frustrated, unvalued, low learner esteem and possibly rebellious?

Finally, it must not be forgotten that this example is only accounting for the occasions when the child initiates the language. Adults also start conversations with children and it is obvious that this adds to the total number of language development opportunities which a child might have in any one day.

ACTIVITY 2.2 – Time: 30 minutes

Using the frameworks in Figures 2.3 and 2.4, write an imaginary script for each, thinking carefully about the sorts of things an adult and child might say in each example. Start each example with the same question in order to explore how it can and cannot be developed. For example:

CHILD: Can I help you to mix that cake, Daddy?

Why is language important to children's thinking?

Do you ever talk to yourself when you are on your own? Most people do at some time or other! There will be different reasons for this at different times. Sometimes it might be a response to something or someone ('If he thinks I'm going to get that report done by tonight he's got another think coming!'). Sometimes it might help to organise our thinking ('Now what was I doing before the phone went? Oh yes! Close windows. Find car keys!').

Young children can often be observed talking to themselves. The narrative that takes place while playing with building bricks, ('Now, I'm going to put two more bricks on there like that and . . . oooops, that was silly. Oh, no! Now they've all fallen down. Oh, no, no, no!'), or the child playing in the water tray, ('Ooooooh! Cold! That's cold, that is. Fill it up. Right to the top. Careful. Careful.'), are actually externalisations of children's thought processes.

We think in language, and therefore if our language is restricted then so is our thinking. When children are involved in learning experiences, whether these are planned or unexpected, the discussion is actually representing more than simple conversation. It is, in fact, assisting them with the organisation and extension just of their thought processes.

We think for many different reasons. For instance, we think in order to:

- plan ahead
- remember back
- solve problems
- analyse in order to understand
- evaluate critically
- choose a response
- interpret meaning
- create new ideas
- create new meaning
- reflect on experiences.

ACTIVITY 2.3 – Time: 10 minutes

List some examples of how you think in each of the ways listed above.
If children are left to their own devices for a large proportion of the time it is easy to see how thinking might not develop to its maximum potential. It is important, therefore, to consider the importance of the relationship between adult and child in order to explore how children's language can be supported in such a way that extends their thinking.

How can adults support and extend children's language?

When we consider the relationship between a preschool child and its primary carer, we know that some forms of interaction are particularly beneficial to a child's language development. These include:

- showing an interest in what the child has to say
- showing respect for what the child knows
- encouraging the child's own ideas
- encouraging the child to explain, describe and evaluate
- demonstrating good models of language
- correcting through example rather than criticism
- encouraging the child to experiment with language
- asking open-ended questions (i.e. which don't just have one correct answer)
- not talking down to or patronising the child
- encouraging the child to demonstrate as he or she talks
- listening well to the child
- drawing attention to texts (e.g. food packets)
- reading and telling stories
- talking about stories and books
- playing with rhymes.

In a one-to-one situation, the adult is often extending the child's language a little beyond his or her previous range. In other words, each time the child learns something new that builds upon what he or she already knows. This idea of extending children's range of language is well documented in the work of Vygotsky

(1978). He suggests that adults who support children's learning should extend that learning beyond the children's *current* levels of achievement towards their *potential* levels of achievement. The area of learning between these two levels Vygotsky has called the 'zone of proximal development'.

How can the educational environment influence children's language?

When children are interacting predominantly with other children of the same age, the language is not necessarily extended as much as when they are interacting with adults – in some cases their peers may even be restricting their language use because they have not yet reached the same levels. When an adult is present, however, the level of interaction can be influenced in a positive way. The one-to-one strategies described above can also be successfully adopted by those who work in early years settings when working with groups and individuals.

Children who attend nursery or school for full days are spending a large part of their time in that environment so it is important that it is stimulating and nurturing of children's language, literacy and learning. If children are going to talk they need something worthwhile to talk about. If they are going to learn to read they need interesting and appealing texts. If they are going to learn to write they need opportunities to experiment and practise for real reasons. All these things need to take place in an environment which is supportive and encouraging so that the children develop a confidence in their own abilities and actively seek to learn. The underlying principles of providing such an environment include:

- good organisation which involves the children
- independence in finding, using and caring for resources
- decision-making opportunities
- time to plan
- time to evaluate
- time to reflect
- experiences which:

  motivate
  build on and extend current knowledge
  challenge
  involve active participation
  involve different types of talk
  have a clear purpose
  require language and literacy in meaningful ways
  are safe
  allow exploration
  allow the children to question
  allow the children to turn to texts
  allow the children to create texts.

Children need to value themselves as learners if they are going to be motivated and positive about learning. They need to be recognised for their achievements and encouraged to learn through their mistakes. This type of environment cannot be created by displays and resources alone. It is created through the attitudes and approaches of the adults in that environment for it is they who can make such a remarkable difference to the quality of children's experiences, learning, progress and welfare.

Language and play

It is a sad fact that even among some educationalists the word 'play' is used to describe a recreational alternative to 'work'. ('When you have finished your work you can play in the home corner.') Perhaps the problem lies in the associated meanings of both words, and a lack of clarity about how we should define 'play' within educational settings.

Enlightened early years teachers know that with careful planning and preparation play and work can actually become one and the same thing. Children can learn an enormous amount through play and much of that learning relates directly to language. Play is a complex subject area, and further reading on this subject is highly recommended. However, just to encourage you to think beyond the surface features of play activities and into the deeper realms of the language learning that might be taking place, Figure 2.5 illustrates some typical activities and the potential they offer for language and literacy. Obviously, in the real situation there would be many more complex learning processes taking place and many sorts of language. Just one example for each experience has been highlighted here.

Experience	Potential for language and literacy learning
Water play	Concept development through exploration
Puppet play	Exploring language of stories
Home corner	Exploring language of adults
Role play corner	Exploring new vocabulary
Paint play	Use of descriptive language
Clay play	Planning
Multilink	Use of mathematical language

Figure 2.5 Language, literacy and play

Integrated and discrete experiences

Language and literacy are woven into the very fabric of all areas of learning in early years settings. Where language activities take place as part of another area of experience (e.g. planning to make models of dinosaurs may require looking at a non-fiction text for information) they are referred to as *integrated approaches to language*.

16

> **ACTIVITY 2.4 – Time: 40 minutes**
>
> *Carry out separate 10-minute observations of three different children engaged in play activities on their own. Try to choose three different types of play for each observation. Make three copies of Activity Sheet 4 'Play and language', one for each observation. On the back of each sheet, make a list of the learning and thought processes that you think were taking place.*

Where language activities take place in their own right (e.g. listening to stories) they are called *discrete language activities*.

This chapter has mainly discussed language and literacy as features of integrated learning. Indeed, an integrated approach is the most natural and meaningful way for young children to learn. But, in order to understand fully the components of language and their implications for supporting adults, it is important also to understand oracy, reading and writing as discrete subject areas, and these are addressed in Chapters 4–8. First of all, however, Chapter 3 looks at assessment, observation, recording and reporting – all vital components in ensuring that children's needs are accurately identified to inform the continuous cycle of planning for learning.

Notes for group leaders

⇨ Have group discussions about:
  - ideas for role play corners
  - ideas for displays
  - ideas for language games
  - language problems encountered
  - examples of good practice
  - examples of discrete language activities
  - examples of integrated language activities
  - experiences of the foundation stage curriculum, early learning goals, National Curriculum, NLS or ALS.

⇨ Activity 2.1 – continue into a whole-group discussion about how the structures of language might change according to the different situations.

⇨ Activity 2.2 – continue in small groups with a comparison and discussion of the scripts.

⇨ Activity 2.4 – develop the Activity through a discussion in pairs about the observations.

⇨ In pairs design an interactive display activity on a given theme.

⇨ In pairs plan a play activity with literacy particularly in mind.

Further reading

Bruce, T. (1996) *Helping Young Children to Play*. London: Hodder and Stoughton.
DfEE (1998) *The National Literacy Strategy Framework for Teaching*. London: DfEE.

DfEE (1999) *The National Literacy Strategy: Additional Literacy Support.* London: DfEE.

DfEE and QCA (1999a) *The National Curriculum for England. English.* London: QCA.

DfEE and QCA (1999b) *Early Learning Goals.* London: QCA.

DfEE and QCA (2000) *Curriculum Guidance for the Foundation Stage.* London: QCA.

Hall, N. (1996) *Listening to Children Think.* London: Hodder and Stoughton.

Moyles, J. (2000) *Playful Children, Inspired Children.* Milton Keynes: Open University Press.

Moyles, J. and Adams, S. (2001) *StEPS: Statements of Entitlement to Play.* Milton Keynes: Open University Press.

Wood, D. (1997) *How Children Think and Learn.* Oxford: Blackwell.

Useful Websites

www.nc.uk.net (National Curriculum)

www.qca.org.uk/(Qualifications and Curriculum Authority)

www.dfee.gov.uk/(Department for Education and Employment)

3 Assessing language and literacy

This chapter discusses reasons for and methods of assessment. Firstly, it describes how supporting adults can make useful contributions to assessment processes through observation, recording and reporting back to teachers, and demonstrates the vital role that informal ongoing assessment plays while actually working with children. It then goes on to provide brief explanations of the national frameworks within which more formal assessment takes place. The chapter also includes a brief section on self-assessment as a tool to help develop reflective and developmental practice.

Individual differences

If all children were predictable in their progress, following the same stages at exactly the same times and responding in identical ways to the same experiences, there would be no need for assessment. Teachers could simply refer to a table of figures and read off the correct level for the child's age. How simple that would be – a production line of identical products!

In reality, of course, children are much more interesting. They are each born with unique genetic profiles and have very different social, emotional and cognitive learning experiences from the day they are born. As a result, they start playgroup, nursery and school not only at different stages of development but bringing with them very diverse sets of attitudes and approaches to learning. If the educational provision in those settings is to be relevant, meaningful and sufficiently challenging for every individual child it is vital that all who work with them fully understand their needs. That understanding comes from careful observation and monitoring and clear communication of information between everyone concerned.

Why is assessment important?

Assessment plays a vital role in providing quality educational experiences for children. Not only does it help us to understand what children can already do and what they need to learn next, it also helps us to measure how well they are progressing. More specifically, teachers need to assess in order to:

- plan appropriate learning experiences
- measure progress
- inform external agencies
- inform the child

- identify levels of support needed
- demonstrate school performance
- measure effectiveness of teaching

- inform the parents
- inform the next teacher or school.

Which children should be assessed?

Assessment is not just for children who are experiencing learning difficulties. All children need to have their progress monitored and their learning needs defined. However, additional diagnostic assessment should also take place for children with particular needs as this provides a more detailed map of which elements need the most focus.

Types of assessment

There are many different types of assessment, each serving slightly different purposes. Here are some of the common terms that you will need to know.

- **summative assessment** – where the child's performance is measured by a score
- **formative or diagnostic assessment** – where the assessment information shows what the child can do and what he or she needs to learn next
- **standardised tests** – where the score can be calculated to show how the child relates to the norm (the test will have been measured on large numbers of children to show 'typical' results)
- **running record/miscue analysis** – a diagnostic reading test where you count and analyse the pattern of mistakes that a child is making while reading aloud in order to identify which strategies need more teaching
- **ongoing informal assessment** – the everyday judgements that teachers and assistants make in order to fine-tune or adapt what has been planned
- **self-evaluation** – where the child reflects on what he or she has achieved, sometimes against targets that he or she has set.

Assessment and planning

Sound assessments of children's abilities enable teachers to plan for:

- *Sequencing* – providing experiences in a developmental order which is appropriate and meaningful to the child and which builds on current abilities;
- *Progression* – ensuring that the child is moving along a pathway of progress and development;
- *Differentiation* – providing experiences and challenges at varying levels for different groups of children and individuals.

Observation

Observation skills are important for all those who work with young children. Looking at the end product of a child's efforts (e.g. a piece of writing) often tells us much less than if we have seen the processes through which the child reached that final stage. Observation is about watching and listening, and these should be happening constantly as you work and play with young children. It is also useful sometimes to observe children from a distance when they are unaware that you are watching. The following questions can provide useful markers for your observations:

- Did the child know what was expected of him/her?
- What did the child already know and understand?
- Was the task planned or unplanned?
- What was the composition of the group?
- Were there equal opportunities for every child to participate?
- What new learning took place?
- What difficulties did the child experience? Why do you think this was?
- Did the child have access to sufficient appropriate resources?

It would be most unfair to assume that a child was not very competent at cutting out, for instance, when in fact the scissors he or she was using were blunt. In other words, observations need to consider factual information rather than making judgemental opinion.

ACTIVITY 3.1 – Time: 5 × 10 minute slots in one week

Make a copy of Activity Sheet 5 'Child observations'. After preliminary discussions with the teacher choose one child to observe. Ten minutes should be spent in each social situation listed on the sheet. These observations might be carried out at various times across a one-week period. Make notes and comments each time about the child's responses, language, behaviour, etc. in each of the different situations. When you have finished collecting your notes, compare them to see if there were differences between the child's responses.

Recording

Recording is necessary to provide evidence of how the child has progressed over a period of time. Records also help with planning. However, the production of records can be time consuming and therefore they should be designed in ways that provide useful and easily accessible information, rather than unnecessary mountains of paper to which no-one ever refers!

Records can be useful for a range of purposes, and the recording format usually varies according to the function of the information. There are long-term profiles of the child which accumulate gradually and include evidence of the child's work. A cooperative approach to this type of record-keeping means that they include a variety of perspectives, including those of the child and parents. This offers a much fuller picture of the child.

Those who assist teachers may also find it useful to make quick records as they work with children in order to be more effective in their reporting back to the teacher. The following checklist provides a reminder of some of the issues involved in recording.

- What function is it serving?
- What do I need to record?
- What can I afford to leave out?
- How can I record?
- Is the recording useful?
- Can the records be easily interpreted?
- Who else can record?
- When is it convenient for the teacher to see the records?

ACTIVITY 3.2 – Time: 30 minutes

Imagine that you are working with four children on a group activity. Design a sheet which would enable you to record useful information quickly in order to report back to the teacher. What general areas of focus might you include (e.g. behaviour, understanding) that could be applied to many different types of activity? Try to use this in a real situation. You will probably need to refine your design.

Reporting

Teachers have a statutory responsibility to report information about each child's progress to a range of different people (e.g. parents, head teacher, government). Supporting adults have a professional responsibility to report to the following.

- *The children.* As you are working with children it is important to feed back to them how they are doing in order to give them encouragement and help them reflect on where to aim for next;
- *The teacher.* It is highly likely that you will have opportunities to observe certain things which the teacher will not see because she or he is working with other children at the time. You therefore need to agree with the teacher how and when you will report back after working with particular groups.

It is also important to remember when not to report! Your knowledge of individual children should not be discussed outside school unless in a professional capacity at a meeting. Parents can become very upset if they feel their child is being discussed with other parents in the playground for example.

National assessment frameworks

It is unlikely that you will be asked to carry out directly any formal assessments. However, you may have to assist in some way and so an understanding of the main national assessment frameworks should be part of your professional training. The key government agendas for the teaching and learning of language and literacy were described in Chapter 2 and assessment is very much an integral part of these.

The foundation stage

The foundation stage begins when children are three-years-old. Ideally they are assessed before they even start attending the early years setting to identify their individual needs. This process closely involves parents and enables prompt and early action to be taken where necessary. Their progress is monitored carefully throughout the foundation stage by measuring the child against carefully defined 'stepping stones'. These stepping stones identify what a child should be able to do (e.g. 'Draw lines and circles using gross motor movement' DfEE 2000, p. 66, para. 2) and examples of what the child might do are provided in the guidelines (e.g. 'Kyle enjoys using paint. He covers the paper using huge brush strokes.' DfEE 2000, p. 66, para. 2). By the end of the foundation stage at the age of five, children are expected to have reached the early learning goals.

The early learning goals and baseline assessment

The early learning goals show what might be reasonably expected for each child to achieve by the end of the foundation stage. In other words they represent the targets towards which the children will be moving by way of the stepping stones. When children start the statutory part of their schooling in Year 1 they are assessed to see how they are achieving in relation to these goals. This baseline helps teachers to measure their progress, from then onwards as they start the National Curriculum.

The National Curriculum

The National Curriculum requires formal assessment of English, maths and science at the end of each Key Stage. These are called National Assessment Tasks and Tests but are often referred to as SATs. At the end of Key Stage 1 the English assessments include a reading activity and a writing activity. (Speaking and listening do not have to be formally assessed.) However, ongoing assessments also provide useful information throughout each academic year as these feed directly into planning and provision. Those who assist teachers will most likely be involved in these. Sometimes, you may be involved in working to an Individual Education Plan or IEP.

Individual Education Plans (IEPs)

The Code of Practice (DfE 1994) requires that children with special educational needs should each have an IEP. This provides details of:

- the nature of the child's learning difficulty
- the action required (e.g. staffing, programmes, external agency help, resources)
- the involvement of parents
- the targets within a specified time frame
- the monitoring and assessment plans
- the arrangements for reviews.

Clearly, assessment, monitoring, recording and reporting play crucial roles in the implementation of IEPs.

Roles and responsibilities

Adults who have a supporting role in early years settings are not responsible for statutory assessment. However, they do have an important part to play in contributing valuable information to the teacher's bank of knowledge. Teaching assistants, for instance, typically spend periods of time daily with children who are finding learning difficult. It is in such a one-to-one or small group situation where there is much information to be gathered; not to make use of the intuitive observations of those adults would be wasting a precious resource which can add to the necessary range of assessment perspectives.

Self-assessment and reflective practice

It is highly beneficial to reflect on what you are doing daily so that you can continue to develop and fine-tune your practice. By observing and critically evaluating yourself at work with children you will become aware of many valuable things and continue to learn in a developmental and constructive way. It is also important to remember that we learn from asking questions! The following activity is designed to help you reflect on your own performance in a specific situation.

ACTIVITY 3.3 – Time: 30 minutes

Make a copy of Activity Sheet 6 'Self-evaluation'. After preliminary discussions with the teacher, arrange to tape a session where you are working with a small group of children. Use the sheet to analyse your input to the session. If possible try to discuss the outcomes with another adult, and try to identify three constructive comments which will help you in the future.

Notes for group leaders

⇨ In small groups compare the findings from Activity 3.1.

⇨ In small groups share and evaluate the designs from Activity 3.2.

⇨ Discuss Activity 3.3 with a partner. Try to build in some constructive peer support.

⇨ Bring in examples of recording formats for record-keeping to compare and discuss.

⇨ In the whole group:

- discuss how often, when and why supporting adults should record information while working with children
- show examples of the stepping stones and get the group to put into a logical sequence
- show and discuss examples of Key Stage 1 National Assessment Tests.

Further reading

Ayers, H. *et al.* (1996) *Assessing Individual Needs*. London: David Fulton Publishers.

Bruce, T. and Bartholomew, L. (1999) *Record Keeping in the Early Years*. London: Hodder and Stoughton.

DfEE amd QCA (2000) *Curriculum Guidance for the Foundation Stage*. London: QCA.

Drummond, M. J. (1993) *Assessing Children's Learning*. London: David Fulton Publishers.

Lawson, H. (1998) *Practical Record Keeping*. London: David Fulton Publishers.

SCAA (1997) *Baseline Assessment Scales*. London: Schools Curriculum and Assessment Authority.

- Speak clearly and audibly with confidence and control and show awareness of the listener, for example by using 'please' or 'thank you'.
- Use language to imagine and recreate roles and experiences.
- Use talk to organise, sequence and clarify thinking, ideas, feelings and events.

If you are working in a setting for 3- and 4-year-olds it is suggested that you look at the stepping stones and practical examples recommended for helping children reach these goals.

Oracy in the National Curriculum

When the original version of the National Curriculum for English was first produced in 1989, many teachers were pleased to see that a whole attainment target was dedicated to speaking and listening. That strand has been maintained in the current revised version, produced in 1999 (DfEE and QCA 1999a). This official recognition of the place of oracy in children's learning demonstrates how important the spoken word is within the language opportunities (such as those in Figure 4.2) which should be provided for young children.

Speaking and listening at Key Stage 1 is prescribed as follows:

> Pupils learn to speak clearly, thinking about the needs of their listeners. They work in small groups and as a class, joining in discussions and making relevant points. They learn to use language in imaginative ways and express their ideas and feelings when working in role and in drama activities.

(DfEE and QCA 1999a, p. 16, para. 2)

Figure 4.2 Making and playing with puppets provides an excellent context for talk

However, if practitioners are to provide appropriate experiences to enable these skills to develop, they need to understand the nature of talk and how it can be organised and managed in educational settings. A good starting point for this is to develop an awareness of the different types of talk.

Different types of talk

As you will have discovered from Activity 4.1, there are different types of talk. When working with early years children a good professional knowledge of the range of talk helps us to stimulate, support and extend children in the development of their speaking and listening skills. Here are some examples of the different types of talk that you may see young children using:

telling stories
reading aloud
exploring
developing ideas
clarifying ideas
predicting
discussing
describing
explaining
justifying (opinions and actions)
comments on talk by others
role play
questioning
decision-making
expanding
evaluating
instructing.

ACTIVITY 4.2 – Time: 20 minutes if writing from memory OR 30 minutes actual observation in your workplace

Make a chart on which to record the different types of talk you have observed in your early years workplace. Use columns to define different curriculum areas of learning, or alternatively the different activity areas available to the children. In each column record the types of talk (e.g. questioning, explaining), and the social context (e.g. group of four, individual). Are there any relationships between certain types of talk and certain activities or curriculum areas? Does any type of talk dominate?

Extending children's spontaneous talk

Almost every interaction in a nursery or early years classroom is an opportunity for developing children's talk. For example, when they are tidying up they can be encouraged to think about how and why they are doing it in the way that they are. However, we cannot assume that just because talk is happening learning is taking place. On the contrary, there are many occasions where the talk might be off-task and the interactions unproductive. So how can those who support the work of teachers ensure that their input is making a valuable contribution towards extending children's learning, and also developing their oracy skills?

You may be interacting with a child in one of several ways:

- *Initiating* – where you make the first move, asking a question or proposing an activity for example.
- *Providing information/resources* – where the child needs something additional, either by his/her own recognition or because you have noticed and stepped in.
- *Giving feedback* – where you are responding to something the child has asked, done or made, etc.
- *Preventing* – where you step in to divert or stop something that is inappropriate or dangerous.

All these types of intervention provide opportunities to extend the child's own talk.

ACTIVITY 4.3 – Time: ongoing

This activity is designed to enable you to reflect upon your own interactions with the children in your workplace. Make a copy of Activity Sheet 8 'Thinking about your talk with children' and place it on a clipboard or file for easy reference. Take one or two questions as a focus each day and record any thoughts on the sheet. The bottom of the sheet includes an 'Action Points' section for you to identify any changes which you may wish to make as a result of your observations.

Promoting good listening skills

Some adults find it hard to listen; sometimes they hear without listening! Children are just the same. The mistake is often made of assuming that because children are sitting quietly on the classroom carpet that they are listening well. Next time you are working with a child after a carpet session, how will you find out if he or she has been listening?

With skilled questioning and checking back one can usually tune in to the level of listening which has taken place. However, when children cannot answer your questions, it is important to consider whether it is because they have not listened or because they have not understood. In actual fact they might have been daydreaming. This 'trancing out' or switching off from the events around us is a highly developed safety mechanism which can sometimes be extremely useful when our brains are tired or in danger of overload. However, it can also be a distracting habit that prevents children from listening and learning – a barrier to communication.

In order to help us understand why children tune out from listening let us consider all the reasons why we, as adults, do the same thing. It might be because we are:

bored

nervous

feeling outstripped by more vociferous group members

feeling unable to express what we feel

fearful of criticism

fearful of saying the wrong thing.

Can you think of any other reasons why you may become detached from a group situation? Taking the examples above, plus any additional ones of your own, can you match these to particular situations in which you have found yourself recently? Understanding the reasons why children are not listening can help us to plan strategies. A child who needs to focus may be set a challenge, for example: 'I'm going to tell the story, then I want you to tell it back to me.' Try not to give too many instructions at once: 'Put your chairs under, go and get your story book, sit on the carpet and share the story with a friend . . .' may just be one instruction too many for some children. Modelling good listening is also important. Are you a good listener yourself? This type of strategic planning can help children to practise and develop where it is most needed.

Planning for talk

Those who support the work of teachers in early years settings are not always directly responsible for the planning of activities, but many are included in team preparations. It is probably helpful, therefore, for you to know some of the main principles which can lie behind the planning of talk activities in order to help you contribute fully to any such team discussions. It is hoped that this will also help you to understand the reasoning behind teachers' thinking. In this way you will develop a more informed awareness of the purpose of planned talk and make an even more valuable contribution in your role as supporting adult to pupils and teachers.

Figure 4.3 illustrates eight important aspects which should be considered when planning talk activities.

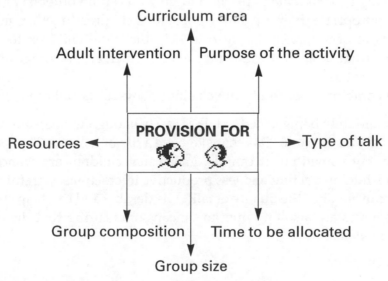

Figure 4.3 Things to consider when planning talk activities

1. Curriculum area. Talk happens right across the curriculum range and opportunities for developing different types of talk can be identified in a clear and purposeful way.

Example: Water tray(science) = explaining.

2. Purpose of the activity. Children are far more likely to become involved in an activity if it has a clear and meaningful purpose.

Example: Cooking (technology) = each child takes turns to give instructions to the next child.

3. Type of talk. If children are to develop a range of skills for communication through talking, it is important to monitor which types of talk they have had opportunities to practise.

Example: Model making (technology) = asking the model-makers questions about their experiences.

4. Time to be allocated. As with all activities, children will wander off-task very quickly if they are bored, struggling, or have finished. However, children will always continue to talk. It is important, therefore, that the purpose and necessity for the talk is monitored time-wise.

Example: Show-and-tell (English) = 5 minutes for child to tell, 5 minutes for questions, 5 minutes reporting back on how much they can remember.

5. Group size. This can vary according to the activity, but can certainly make a difference to the quality of input. Pairs work well, a trio can involve an observer/recorder dynamic, fours tend to need more rules. Large group discussions need very clear ground rules and these are best established in consultation with the children themselves. Too long in a large group situation can become frustrating for many children, hence the 'restlessness on the carpet' syndrome.

Example: Story-making (English) = make up a story in pairs; split up and go and tell a new partner your story.

6. Group composition. Self-selected friendship groups are sometimes appropriate, but occasionally it is valuable to place children with certain others. For example, it is sometimes appropriate to group all the vociferous children together, not just to give the others more of a chance, but also to help the vocal children to practise their listening and social skills. Be aware of the effects which group composition has upon the quality of the talk.

Examples of combinations: ability, mixed ability, boys, girls, talkative, shy.

7. Resources. Merely being asked to talk is rarely enough to keep any group on task for a sufficiently useful time. Talk tends to have a life of its own. This can be exciting and creative, but sometimes it can also mean that children are wandering off the learning track into distracting and less productive interactions. Careful consideration of resources can enhance the quality of talk considerably and can help children to stay on-task. Resources are also an important means of ensuring that the children have something to talk about!

Resources can be divided broadly into three categories:

1. stimulus resources
2. support resources
3. recording resources.

Stimulus resources are those that help get the talk started. For instance pictures, artefacts, stories, visitors. It is difficult for children to learn how to use the powers of description if they are not given interesting objects and experiences to describe.

Support resources are resources which provide the talk with some form of framework. Examples might include a shell to hold when taking turns to talk, instructions to follow, prompt cards and use of telephones (Figure 4.4).

Recording resources can be a way of providing a goal or end-product for the talk. Examples might include large sheets of paper and felt-tips for brainstorming (in pictures or words as appropriate) or making lists of things needed to make a model following discussion of the subject. Recording in this way provides children with cues and support for their talk.

Example: Measuring distance of toy cars down a ramp (maths) = discuss and record the distances in order by drawing them on a prepared sheet.

8. Adult intervention. Interventions can be made in many ways including listening, questioning, instructing and reminding, to name but a few. Planned intervention can help to ensure that the talk stays on-task, rather than waiting until a hub-bub arises to attract you over to the activity.

Example: Describing their houses (geography) = say that you are not going to join in for the first five minutes, but watch to see how well they are listening to each other. Then ask questions and direct the next part of the task.

Figure 4.4 Using the telephone as a framework for talk

Organising and managing talk

You will all recognise children you have worked with who are often reluctant to talk, or who rarely take a turn in large groups. Certain management techniques can help you plan to overcome this. One such technique is sometimes called 'rainbowing', where children working in groups are each given a colour. They then move into a new group, along with children who have the same colour, where they have to report back. Reporting back, or explaining/describing to a partner, can also be a good way to encourage quieter children.

ACTIVITY 4.4 – Time: 30 minutes

Imagine that you are assigned to work with a group on 'Homes and Houses'. The teacher wants the children to make decisions about a range of options for house design. Make a resource that you think will help to keep the children on-task and which will influence this type of decision-making talk.

The resources, challenges and goals provided by adults can motivate the right sorts of talk, and are therefore also useful management mechanisms. In other words, if children are going to engage in a range of talk activities they need appropriate purposes for their talk supported by relevant resources as discussed in more detail previously in this chapter.

Last but not least, talking about talk helps children to understand the significance of what they are doing. There is much value in drawing attention to the types of talk as they are being used and discussing the qualities which are required in different situations. Praising children for the ways in which they are speaking is just as appropriate as praising them for their reading and writing. Likewise with listening. If you make it clear to children that you value their turn-taking behaviour, for example, they are more likely to demonstrate this on future occasions. Perhaps most importantly, the children will grow to recognise the importance and power of their own oracy skills.

Notes for group leaders

⇨ Discuss Activity 4.1 with the whole group.

⇨ Discuss Activity 4.2 in pairs.

⇨ Use partners to give feedback and constructive suggestions after Activity 4.3.

⇨ Look at the stepping stones and examples on page 48 of the *Curriculum Guidance for the Foundation Stage* (DfEE and QCA 2000) and share other actual examples that have been observed by group members (whole group).

⇨ Look at page 16 in the National Curriculum Order for English (DfEE and QCA 1999a) and discuss/share observations of how children have demonstrated some of these competencies (whole group).

⇨ Discuss when it is not appropriate to intervene in children's talk (whole group).

⇨ Discuss the issues around 'correcting' children's speech (whole group).

⇨ In groups of three, brainstorm ideas on how you might encourage certain types of talk in the following situations: water play, maths, art.

Further reading

Edwards,V. (1995) *Speaking and Listening in Multilingual Classrooms*. Reading: Reading and Language Information Centre.

Fidge, L. (1992) *The Essential Guide to Speaking and Listening*. Dunstable: Folens.

Grugeon, E. *et al.* (1998) *Teaching Speaking and Listening in the Primary School*. London: David Fulton Publishers.

Holderness, J. and Lalljee, B. (eds) (1998) *An Introduction to Oracy*. London: Cassell.

Williams, B. (2000) *Skills for Early Years: Speaking and Listening*. Leamington Spa: Scholastic.

5 The complexity of reading

This chapter explores the processes of reading in order to help you understand what children need to learn, and how they develop as readers. The model of reading provided by The National Literacy Strategy Framework for Teaching (DfEE 1998) is explained and the chapter also briefly describes the curriculum guidelines for the foundation stage (DfEE and QCA 2000), the early learning goals (DfEE and QCA 1999b) and the National Curriculum level descriptions (DfEE and QCA 1999a).

The importance of reading

Whenever standards in education are discussed, reading is usually at the centre of the debate. When parents express concern to teachers about their child's progress it is more often than not about his or her reading. When the Government expresses concern about levels of pupils' performance it usually includes their performance in reading. It is easy to see why reading has such an important place in our society-not only is it central to learning across the curriculum, it is also an important skill that is required every day by the majority of people (see Figures 5.1, 5.2 and 5.3).

When we stop to think of the tremendous range of texts that we read automatically it becomes apparent just how significant reading is in our lives, even if we don't

Figure 5.1 We are surrounded by text!

Figure 5.2 Supermarkets are rich in print

Figure 5.3 Symbols are also contributing to children's concepts of print

regularly read novels! There are the texts that we actively seek out to read for the purposes of our work, our leisure and to perform many important operations within the running of our lives. Then there are the texts that confront us continuously in and around the environment. When we watch television we see text, and computers, of course, generate text and hyper-text. Even mobile phones can send and receive text messages!

ACTIVITY 5.1 – Time: 10 minutes

Think about some of the places you have visited during the past few days. This might include work, college, shops, bus station, train station, cinema or the doctor's waiting room. On a blank sheet of paper, jot down all the examples of text that you can remember from those situations.

Do we read everything in the same way?

Having identified examples of the texts that you encounter every day, let us now consider how you approach those texts. Imagine all the mail that might be delivered through your door on a typical day. The first envelope is your telephone bill. You know this before you have even opened it because of the type, colour and size of print, and also the recognisable logo – you have already used certain reading skills to make sense of this visual information. What do you do when you have unfolded the papers inside the envelope? Do you start at the top left-hand corner and read systematically from left to right down the page until you have finished? Almost certainly, the answer to this question will be 'no'! It is much more likely that you scan straight down to the total to see how much you owe. Consider how people read a menu. Some may look at the wine list on the back page first so that they can enjoy a drink while choosing the meal. Others may look at the puddings first, or some may be looking just at the prices to spot the cheapest deal. A train timetable involves quite complex cross-referencing whereas a set of self-assembly instructions needs to be read systematically in sequential order. If you are reading a non-fiction book you are quite likely to refer to the contents page and also the index, whereas you are unlikely to read down the list of chapter titles of a romantic novel, unless, of course, you want some clues about the story in advance! In other words, we read different types of texts in different ways, and sometimes this requires different strategies or skills.

ACTIVITY 5.2 – Time: 20 minutes

Using Activity Sheet 9 'What do I do when I read?', think carefully about the different types of texts listed. Next, taking each one at a time, try to recall exactly what you do when you read that type of text. This might include such things as where you start, how carefully you read it, the parts you ignore and the order in which you read it, how easily you recognise the words, etc.

By focusing on the different ways in which you read you will start to develop an awareness of just how complicated the reading process is. Early years children are engaged in developing a wide range of skills, knowledge and understanding about reading to enable them to take part effectively in this process. If you are going to support them in ways that encourage this development, it is important for you to understand what is actually taking place when readers read.

What do we do when we read?

When you started to read this chapter how did you look at the text? Did you look at the individual letters and build up the sounds, taking each word separately to construct the sentences? Probably not. It is more likely that you recognised whole words and moved along the lines of writing in chunks. Speed readers are even able to read down the central column of a page taking in whole lines of text at once.

Experienced readers rarely need to 'sound out' the letters to build up a word as early readers do. They have developed the skills and knowledge to see and identify whole words as single units. However, if they encounter a strange word that they have not seen before (for example a foreign place name) they will probably need to go back to building up the letters into sounds, while at the same time drawing upon their knowledge of letter patterns from more familiar words that are similar in order to help with pronunciation and emphasis.

To help you experience how that works, here is a simple task. Look at the word below and try to say it out loud.

KNEBEVIGHT

You probably said something which sounded like 'neebvite'. Why did you not pronounce the K, the second E, and the G and H? You already know words with these silent letters and patterns in them and so you transferred the rules across. In other words you used your knowledge of letter shapes, letter sounds and spelling rules to say the word.

So you have read the word aloud, but have you really read it? No! All you have done is translated shapes into sounds. At the moment there is no meaning. Let us look at the word again in a sentence.

SALLY PULLED HER KNEBEVIGHT

How many possible meanings can you think of for this strange word? We know now that the word is a noun because of its relationship with the other words in the sentence. But is this in fact a sentence? Where is the full stop? Let's have some more clues.

SALLY PULLED HER KNEBEVIGHT ON

The addition of one more word makes an enormous difference to our understanding of the word, and yet still there is no clear meaning. Nor is there yet a full stop.

SALLY PULLED HER KNEBEVIGHT ON TO KEEP HERSELF WARM.

That narrows it down a bit, and yet even so the word could still have a variety of meanings – coat, hat, duvet . . . We have arrived at the end of the sentence because now we have a full stop. However, we still need more information in order to understand the meaning of our mystery word. If there was a picture we might be able to see what Sally was pulling on. In the absence of a picture, let us look further on in the text.

SHE WRAPPED IT AROUND HER NECK SEVERAL TIMES

Is there an outside chance that the knebevight could be a pet python? Read on!

AND ALTHOUGH THE COLOURS OF HER FAVOURITE FOOTBALL TEAM CLASHED WITH HER HAT, SHE WAS TRULY GRATEFUL FOR ITS PROTECTION FROM THE BITING WIND.

I think we can be pretty sure now that the knebevight is a scarf!

In order to read those two sentences for meaning the following strategies had to be used:

- divide the word into chunks
- build up letter sounds by applying knowledge of other words and rules
- connect the relationship of the words grammatically
- use the context for clues.

For the purposes of this very simple exercise these strategies took place one at a time because the text was unfolded to you in parts whereas under normal reading conditions the effective reader employs all those strategies almost simultaneously when encountering new words. An early reader, however, has not yet developed the skills to employ this range of strategies in such a sophisticated way. Learning to do this requires teaching, practice and experience of a range of texts and strategies.

ACTIVITY 5.3 – Time: 15 minutes

Find or make a copy of Activity Sheet 10 'Analysing your reading strategies', but cover it up immediately with a sheet of paper! Read the instructions at the top then uncover one piece of text at a time to analyse what strategies you have to use to decipher these rather unusual texts.

Categories of engagement with the text

By now, you will have realised that when we read we employ different sorts of strategies in order to make sense of the text. Let us now look at these strategies more closely. The strategies that we use when we read fall into four categories illustrated in Figure 5.4.

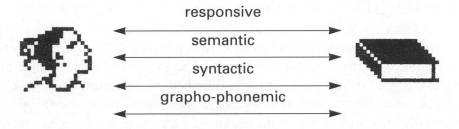

Figure 5.4 The four categories of engagement

The diagram represents the reader, the text and the four types of connection that take place between the two. These are called *categories of engagement* because they are pathways which 'engage' or 'connect' the reader in some way with the text.

1. Responsive engagement

This type of engagement is where the reader is responding to what he or she has read. At the very early levels of reading this might include a toddler pointing to a picture and laughing. At a more developed stage this could mean a child talking about why he or she does not like a certain character and predicting what is going to happen next. Response is more than understanding because it brings to the text the reader's own experiences and individuality.

2. Semantic engagement

Semantic engagement is the level at which the reader is making meaning from the text. It is about understanding what has been read. This involves getting clues from pictures, understanding the meanings of words and also how the words are organised, for example 'the cat was on the hat' means something different from 'the hat was on the cat'.

3. Syntactic engagement

The organisation of words in a sentence is known as the syntax. This is guided by grammatical rules and punctuation. Understanding these conventions helps the child to decipher and understand the text. For example, full stops give us important information to help us make sense of what we read.

4. Grapho-phonemic engagement

The 'graph' part means visual and the 'phon' part means sound. Quite simply, this aspect of reading is about seeing the shapes of the letters and transforming them into the sounds which make words. It is often referred to as 'decoding' the text.

ACTIVITY 5.4 – Time: 10 minutes

Refer back to the notes you made during Activity 5.3 and try to allocate each of the strategies you used to one of the four categories of engagement.

By going through this process you will notice that there is overlap and interweaving between the categories of engagement. It is most important to remember that they work simultaneously when the reader is experienced. However, when children are in the early stages of learning to read, they are more likely to use strategies in isolation. For example, children may read in a 'robot-voice' from their books without any errors and yet when they reach the end they do not remember what they have read. In other words, they have been decoding, but not understanding. There are several important things to remember about the four categories of engagement.

- They are not learned in a special order one after the other.
- Individual readers will use them in different proportions.
- Some children need support within one category more than others.
- The effective reader uses them in combination.

The National Literacy Strategy model of reading

The NLS (DfEE 1998) provides a similar model from which teachers are advised to teach the strategies of reading. These strategies are referred to as 'searchlights', each of which sheds light on the text for the reader. The four searchlights are:

- Phonics (sounds and spelling)
- Grammatical knowledge
- Word recognition and graphic knowledge
- Knowledge of context.

During the Literacy Hour children are taught systematically to discriminate between the separate sounds in words, learn letters and letter combinations, sound out words and blend the separate parts and write words by combining patterns with sounds. Their knowledge of the grammatical structures combined with their understanding of what they are reading will also assist in ensuring success. In other words, focused teaching of the different strategies is provided so that a balanced operation can be achieved. The National Curriculum also stresses that activities should be meaningful and stimulating to the children rather than mechanical decontextualised tasks.

Developmental progress in reading

Not only should you be aware of the strategies that children need for reading, you will also need to understand the developmental nature of reading. Some years ago, early years teachers were trained to teach what were then called 'pre-reading' or 'reading readiness' skills. These included activities such as picture matching, listening, sight recognition and memory games and were provided in order to 'prepare' children for reading. During the 1950s children would only be given reading books once they knew enough letters and sound to be able to decode those books.

Today, such games continue to be a useful part of children's learning, but the notion that this is 'pre-reading' has been rejected. Instead, it is now recognised that reading skills develop on a continuum rather than the children reaching a point where suddenly they are readers when the day before they were not! For example, the three-year-old who sits with an adult and talks about the story and points to the pictures, predicting what comes next, is in the early stages of reading. This type of involvement with texts is recognised as an important foundation because children are now considered to be well on their way to reading (and writing) before they start to decode text. This stage is known as emergent literacy.

The emergent reader is the child who knows what books are for, who enjoys stories, can talk about books, and is already aware of the function of print. It is staggering how much children already know about reading by the time they start nursery or playgroup. The word TESCO on a carrier bag, the STOP sign at the end of the road, the shopping list, the birthday card all carry particular messages that are understood by many young children. Earlier in this chapter you were asked to focus on the variety of print in your life. Such a stimulating print environment has a profound effect on the early learning of young children and it should not be ignored because it provides a healthy basis for ongoing learning.

As the child begins to learn more systematically about the components of reading, (the letters, sounds, words and grammar,) he or she begins to move towards becoming a supported reader. At this stage the child is showing an interest in tackling some print with the help of a more experienced reader. He or she will look at books for pleasure but needs help to read unfamiliar texts.

Gradually the child develops into a fluent reader as he or she builds up a knowledge of how texts work. The child will tend to revisit familiar texts that can be read with confidence, but also approach new texts with increasing skill and confidence. At this stage, the child will start to read some parts of some texts silently.

Eventually, the child will develop into an independent reader. Typically, a child at this stage will be choosing texts from a range of sources, will understand what is read and be able to discuss it with reference to the text. The child will also be starting to read 'between the lines' (inferential reading) for hidden meanings.

Figure 5.5 Reading and writing are closely interlinked

Reading starts from birth

There are many projects and programmes now that provide parents with early story books when their baby is born. Hearing the rhythms and structures of story language and, perhaps most importantly, learning to enjoy books, from early in a child's life has been shown to make an important difference to children's progress in reading and writing later on (Figure 5.5). However, children will have a range of home experiences prior to joining a more formal educational setting. They will also have different birth months and inherited predispositions to learning. All these things mean that children are starting at different points on the reading continuum. The curriculum guidelines for the foundation stage (DfEE and QCA 2000) offer, for the first time in educational history in England, a carefully structured framework to provide all children with a rich and stimulating learning environment that will prepare as many as possible to respond positively and confidently to the National Curriculum provision once they are five.

Government guidelines on progression in reading

The early learning objectives to be reached by the time children are five are to:

- Explore and experiment with sounds, words and texts
- Retell narratives in the correct sequence, drawing on language patterns of stories
- Read a range of familiar and common words and simple sentences independently
- Know that print carries meaning and, in English, is read from top to bottom and left to right
- Show an understanding of stories, such as main character, sequence of events, and openings, and how much information can be found in non-fiction texts to answer questions about where, who, why and how.

(DfEE and QCA 2000, p. 62)

A further goal area, linking sounds to letters, relates to both reading and writing.

The curriculum guidance (DfEE and QCA 2000) provides stepping stone stages and examples of activities for practitioners to provide. These include fun opportunities to listen to, read, play with, retell, enact and generally explore stories. Making books and talking about books are also important. Likewise, looking at and interacting with other texts such as labels, menus, telephone directories plays a vital role in familiarising children with the purpose of a range of texts. Rhyme and sound games, later linking these to the visual shapes of letters, are helping children to develop an awareness of the relationship between graphemes (letter shapes and letter patterns) and phonemes (sounds). It has already been emphasised earlier in this book that speaking, listening, reading and writing are very closely interlinked. So, for example, when children are talking about stories this is also helping their understanding of story language and how texts work, which in turn is developing early reading skills.

Once children start statutory schooling, the National Curriculum Attainment Targets provide level descriptions for the different Programmes of Study. It may be helpful for you to be familiar with those for reading (remembering that Level 2 is the national average for the end of Year 2):

> **Level 1:** Pupils recognise familiar words in simple texts. They use their knowledge of simple letters and sound–symbol relationships in order to read words and to establish meaning when reading aloud. In these activities they sometimes require support. They express their response to poems, stories and non-fiction by identifying aspects they like.

> **Level 2:** Pupils' reading of simple texts shows understanding and is generally accurate. They express opinions about major events or ideas in stories, poems and non-fiction. They use more than one strategy, such as phonic, graphic, syntactic and contextual, in reading unfamiliar words and establishing meaning.

> **Level 3:** Pupils read a range of texts fluently and accurately. They read independently, using appropriate strategies to establish meaning. In responding to fiction and non-fiction they show understanding of the main points and express preferences. They use their knowledge of the alphabet to locate books and find information.

> (DfEE and QCA 1999a, p. 56)

Helping the strugglers

Despite these clear stages of progression, you will already be aware that children do not necessarily develop at the same pace for all kinds of reasons. Assistants are often employed to work with small groups of readers who need a particular focus, and sometimes with individual struggling readers. Chapter 6 goes on to look more closely at how you might support children in small groups, including those who are behind with reading.

Developing your professional knowledge

Clearly, it is beyond the scope of this book to provide you with a full course on the teaching and learning of reading! The aim of this chapter was to raise your awareness of how complex reading is and the developmental stages through which children need to pass. You will need to extend your knowledge of reading and how it is taught even further and the books recommended at the end of this chapter will provide additional levels of understanding.

Notes for group leaders

⇨ In pairs, sort the examples from Activity 5.2 into 'types' of reading.

⇨ Activity 5.3 could be conducted with the whole group by making an overhead projector copy of Activity Sheet 10 'Analysing your reading strategies'.

⇨ Discussions about the nature of support will be useful, as will opportunities to experience and feed back on giving support to other group members. Photocopy a piece of text (if possible with pictures) onto an overhead projector skin then turn the skin the wrong way and make paper copies so that the text is back-to-front. Get the group to work in pairs, one taking the role of supporting adult helping the other who is the reader. After five minutes of 'reading' ask them to reflect on the strategies they were using to decipher and understand the text and what was helpful from their partner. Discuss as a large group.

⇨ In groups of three, make a collection of examples of print that are not on paper and make a display.

⇨ In groups of four, brainstorm ideas for linking reading and writing in a nursery class.

Further reading

Bielby, N. (1998) *How to Teach Reading. A Balanced Approach*. Leamington Spa: Scholastic.
Browne, A. (1998) *A Practical Guide to Teaching Reading in the Early Years*. London: Paul Chapman.
Clarke, M. (1994) *Young Literacy Learners – How We Can Help Them*. Leamington Spa: Scholastic.
Layton, L. *et al.* (1997) *Sound Practice: Phonological Awareness in the Classroom*. London: David Fulton Publishers.
Oakhill, J. *et al.* (1999) *Reading Development and Teaching Reading*. Oxford: Blackwell.

6 Supporting children's reading activities

The previous chapter aimed to increase your understanding of reading processes and developmental stages. This chapter attempts to link that theoretical knowledge to the everyday practicalities of working with children. It examines the relationship skills that can contribute to the quality of support offered by adults to children when they are engaged in reading activities. The nature of this support is then discussed within the context of different reading activities commonly found in nurseries and early years classrooms.

Developing quality relationships

Those who assist in early years settings spend much of their time supporting children's reading across a wide range of activities. These include working individually with one child, working with different sized groups and sometimes reading stories to the whole class. The quality of the relationship between child and supporting adult can have a significant effect on the productivity of those activities. Not only does it influence the development of the child's reading it can also affect how the child perceives itself as a reader.

To begin, let us focus on what we mean by support. Figure 6.1 illustrates four key qualities that you can bring to supporting children's reading.

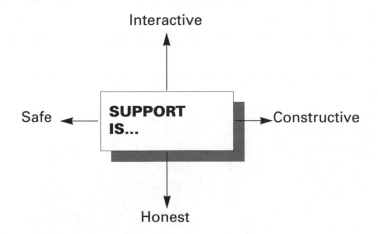

Figure 6.1 Components of support

These four components encompass all the important qualities required to support children with their reading. Let us look at each in turn.

1. Support is interactive

To be a passive onlooker is to miss opportunities for helping the child. You are a valuable resource for learning. However, advice, guidance and information can be offered in many different ways and it is important that you do not regard yourself as a 'knowledge machine'. The support needs to be a two-way process so that you and the child are responding to each other. The following points should be considered:

- How can I find out what the child needs to know?
- How can the child be encouraged to ask questions?
- How can the child learn from my example?
- How does the child perceive my explanations?
- How can I check that the child understands what has been discussed?
- How can I be a good reading role model?
- Do I leave enough space for the child to respond?

2. Support is constructive

A constructive approach to learning means building on what is already there in a positive and developmental way. When children share their ideas and expertise with an adult they are placing great trust in that adult. For some children that can be quite difficult because they feel they are laying themselves open to criticism, particularly if they do not get much support at home. If we start from the sound base of a child's current expertise we can always find a positive focus. Children respond more effectively to praise than criticism, and building on their expertise has the additional benefit of boosting their self-esteem.

- Do I always 'pounce' immediately on the mistakes?
- If so, what impact does this have on the child?
- Am I aware of individual differences between children's abilities and needs?
- How can I identify what the child is already doing well?
- How can I praise sincerely?
- How can I offer constructive feedback?
- Do I give children the opportunity to revisit and practise the areas of feedback?

3. Support is honest

Honesty is important in any relationship. Children soon know if an adult is patronising them or giving praise where praise is not due. Being honest in the reading relationship is not necessarily about pointing out all the mistakes, but it can be about the following:

- Correcting the necessary number of errors in a constructive way
- Praising specifics rather than making general statements
- Giving your own opinions about the book you are sharing
- Disagreeing with the child in an OK way!
- Allowing the child to disagree with you in an OK way!

- Giving positive feedback before identifying areas for development
- Asking the child for his or her opinions
- Encouraging children to be honest with each other
- Talking about your own mistakes
- Talking about the books you read at home.

4. Support is safe

If children are going to try their very best and are determined to succeed they have to take risks. If they are afraid to try an unknown word because they are worried they might get it wrong their learning will be held back. However, if they trust the adults with whom they work they will be more likely to experiment and explore, and in this way they will be constantly pushing out the boundaries of their learning experiences and achievements. Examples of this might include the books they choose, the ideas they express, disagreeing with your opinions about books, asking questions, setting their own targets and so on.

- How do I show children that I respect their expertise?
- Do I encourage children to take risks (e.g. have a go at a strange word)?
- Do I ensure that children are comfortable?
- Do I give children the time they need?
- Do I provide opportunities for children to discuss their own learning?
- Do I provide opportunities for children to set and review their own targets?
- How do I show children that I value their efforts?

ACTIVITY 6.1 – Time: 15 minutes

Reflect on the support that you give to the children in your care in three situations – with individuals, small groups and the whole class (if appropriate). On a sheet of paper write down what you consider to be your strengths in each situation and then identify the areas which you would like to develop. If possible, try to discuss these notes with an adult who can support you in making these changes.

Listening to children read

Working with individual readers is a task that dominates the work of many assistants and parent helpers. There is sometimes a danger that this can become a regimented chore when a list has to be completed, and the children have to go through a production line! Therefore, let us stop to consider that for the child this is an important time and a time that deserves quality input from you. It is worth remembering that each child will bring to this experience a different agenda. Here are some examples:

> 'Oh, good! It's my turn!'
> 'Oh, no! It's my turn!'
> 'Why does she always call me when I'm doing something good?'
> 'I hope I can read properly today.'

'I'm frightened that I may get it wrong.'
'I need extra help because I'm thick.'

You can probably think of many more. The agenda will be influenced, to a large extent, by the way the child has experienced this time with you previously. In other words if you were cross with the child for mispronouncing words yesterday he or she is unlikely to feel very enthusiastic about repeating the process today.

There are three questions that you need to consider when working with individual readers. How can you ensure that the experience is enjoyable for the child? How can you ensure that the child is learning more about reading during this time? How can you feed back information that will be useful to the teacher?

The following suggestions are provided to give you some guidelines that apply equally to situations where you might be reading to a child who has not yet started to decode text.

Ensuring that the experience is enjoyable for the child

Putting children at their ease is not merely about being a kind person. It is about creating an atmosphere in which children want to learn and feel motivated to work to their optimum ability.

- Be sensitive in your timing.
- Try to invite the child to share a book with you rather than summoning him or her.
- Put the child at ease.
- Discuss the book he or she has chosen to read before asking the child to read it.
- Do not rush the child – leave time for self-correction.
- Respond to what the child is doing well and be encouraging.

Ensuring that the experience is a valuable learning time for the child

Part of the skill of extending children's learning is to select appropriately. Obviously if you attempted to do all the things listed below the poor child would hardly find time to read! Consider carefully, in consultation with the teacher, what the child can already do in order to identify which of the interventions below are appropriate. Interrupting the flow can be unproductive if it is frustrating the child's efforts and distracting his or her concentration.

- Let the child hold the book and turn the pages, even if you are doing the reading.
- Talk together about the book features (cover, front, back and author, etc.).
- Talk together about the pictures.
- Talk together about the characters.
- Talk together about the language features (letters, words, spaces, etc.).
- Talk together about experiences relating to the story (e.g. the child's pet).
- Encourage the child to look for clues when reading.
- Encourage the child to build up the sounds of words.
- Encourage the child to read for meaning in sections (discuss as you go).
- Allow time to revisit or reread areas of uncertainty.
- Read along with the child if he or she needs support.
- Where you are doing all the reading, encourage the child to predict or guess some of the words as you read.

- Encourage the child to predict and explain.
- Praise specific strategies rather than just saying 'Very good!' (e.g. 'I liked the way you chopped up that word to help you work it out!').

Giving useful feedback to the teacher

If you spend a period of quality learning time with any one child you are bound to collect vital information that could prove useful to the teacher. Nurseries and schools vary in the ways they record reading time, but try to consider the following points when feeding back information.

- Make your comments informative. 'Jason read well' tells me nothing. Does this mean that Jason read fluently, understood what he read, read with expression or read new words? A comment such as 'Jason is starting to read the start of the sentence again to find extra clues when he gets stuck on a word' is far more useful.
- The mistakes that children make when they are reading can be extremely useful. Try to note these down if there is an obvious pattern. For example, 'Seems to have a problem with vowels when they are in the middle of words.'
- Take note of the child's attitude towards reading and books.

ACTIVITY 6.2 – Time: 40 minutes

Please check with the teacher before doing this activity. Make a copy of Activity Sheet 11 'Getting to know a reader' and arrange to share a book with the child that you and the teacher have chosen. Try to make this part of your usual routine so that the child feels comfortable. You will probably need to do most of the recording afterwards, although where writing in reading record books is part of the normal practice then it should be all right to jot notes down during the activity. It is probably wise to do this exercise with a range of children so that one child does not feel he or she has been singled out. It will certainly be useful for you to compare different children.

Figure 6.2 Children love looking at photos and these can be used to make interesting books for shared reading

Paired reading

Paired reading was developed in the 1970s and refers to a specific type of reading partnership. It is a partnership in which the child reads to the adult, the adult reads to the child and sometimes the two read simultaneously. The important feature is that the child is in control of this and can decide who reads and when. This is usually signalled by nudging elbows or patting on the hand. Putting the child in the driving seat like this can be extremely reassuring to those who lack confidence with their reading. The adult is there to provide support as and when the child needs it.

Shared reading

Shared reading is the term applied to two people enjoying a book together. This might mean two children of the same age (Figure 6.2), an older child and a younger child or a child and an adult. The reading can be shared as decided by the children, but the central feature of shared reading is the booktalk that also takes place during this time. Talking about books plays an important role in the development of readers (Figure 6.3). Discussing the pictures, the characters, the action, the author's style, predicting, explaining, questioning, empathising, comparing and so on all enrich children's understanding of and responses to books.

Figure 6.3 Children benefit from talking about what they are reading

Group reading

In recent years group reading has become extremely popular with teachers and children. It is particularly effective for older children who are starting to read independently, but benefit from the supported framework provided by reading in a group. Each child has a copy of one text and he or she takes turns reading aloud while the rest of the group follow the text in their own copy. This can be varied by, for example, reading in unison with or without the adult, reading parts, reading a sentence each. Teaching points can be made during the process such as new vocabulary, reinforcement or repetition of phonemes, use of expression and so on. The practice is often extended into follow-up activities, which provide the children with opportunities to explore particular aspects of language using the story or play as a starting point.

Guided reading

This is an approach introduced by the NLS (DfEE 1998) in which a group of children at the same reading level read from the same text but each at their own pace. As with group reading the adult uses the time to teach and correct both individuals and the group. Hearing five children read at a different pace simultaneously requires great skill, and this approach is not as popular as group reading because many teachers feel uncomfortable with children reading on while they are focusing on an individual. It is, however, an efficient use of adult time although it has been argued by some that a 'production-line approach' can be discouraging to children, particularly struggling readers.

Reading games

Reading games are not only an enjoyable activity for children, they can also be an effective resource for learning. Reading skills and strategies can be placed within the context of a game to provide an opportunity to repeat, revisit and practise in ways that are enjoyable and meaningful.

Many types of games are commercially available, but it is also possible to make games. Assistants on the Specialist Teacher's Assistant (STA) course at Oxford Brookes University School of Education were asked to make a reading game using early years fiction as a starting point and theme. The design, making and evaluation of the game constituted one of the assignments for their course. The ideas they came up with were inspiring! They included game boards (*Rosie's Walk* by Pat Hutchins), cloze procedure (*We're Going on a Bear Hunt* by Michael Rosen), matching (*Dear Zoo* by Rod Campbell), sorting, rhyming snap (*Each Peach Pear Plum* by J. and A. Ahlberg), sentence making (*The Snowman* by Raymond Briggs) and many more (Figure 6.4).

Trialling the games with groups of children was also an exciting part of this work. The enjoyment and learning was evident, and they were also able to make adjustments to their games based on observations of how they worked in practice. Needless to say the teacher mentors were delighted with these additional resources for their classrooms, and the next phase of the project was to encourage the assistants

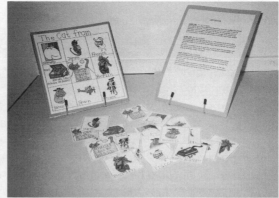

Figure 6.4 These reading games, using picture books as starting points, were made by STA course students at Oxford Brookes University

to lead groups of volunteer parents in the making of games for different classrooms according to the needs specified by the teachers.

Using stories as starting points for games has many benefits. The game can be planned to introduce and use specific skills, but in addition there are golden opportunities for talking about the book, characters, plot, author and so on. Games relating to specific books encourage children to use the language of those books and contribute to the literary environment.

Supporting children during the Literacy Hour

Every school tends to approach the Literacy Hour slightly differently according to their children, school organisation, resources and so on. You may be asked to sit with a child during the whole-class time to ensure he or she is concentrating or add further explanation while the teacher is talking. The Literacy Hour is designed to use best practice in terms of clear instruction. This includes: directing; demonstrating; modelling (showing a child by doing something yourself first); scaffolding (supporting alongside while the child attempts something, before you withdraw to let him or her have a go independently); questioning; explaining to clarify; guiding/encouraging exploration; discussing/challenging; and listening and responding. It is important to have high (but realistic) expectations of the children, work at a good pace and encourage discussion. It is also vital that you are clear about what is expected of you so that you feel confident about your own knowledge.

ACTIVITY 6.3 – Time: 6 hours

Part 1 – Making a reading game
Using children's literature as a starting point for activities in the classroom is just one way of enriching the literary environment in schools. Bearing this in mind, you are recommended to make a reading game that is based upon a picture book. It can take any form you wish – e.g. board game, card game, tape, etc. Think carefully about which specific aspects of reading the game addresses. Try to imagine the processes that a child will go through as he or she plays the game. These may not be the same as adult processes. It would be wise to include an instruction card in the game so that other adults will understand how to use it.

Try to ensure that any text and pictures within the game are clear and professionally reproduced. You may wish to use word processing for this rather than handwritten print. If you are able to laminate the game it is likely to last considerably longer than if it is used in its unprotected form.

Part 2 – A written analysis of your game
This is not an explanation of how to play the game, but a justification of the methods employed. How is the game going to support the children who play it? What skills is it helping to develop? You may wish to support your explanations with references to background reading, but this is not essential. Ideally, you will be able to show this to your teacher or group leader in order to receive some feedback. If this is not possible, it is nevertheless a useful process to evaluate your work for yourself. Perhaps you could exchange feedback with a fellow assistant who would also like to try this activity. The following questions might help you to do this:

- *Does the game clearly address specific reading skills?*
- *Have I demonstrated a good understanding of those skills?*
- *Are the playing instructions clear?*
- *Is the game well made and attractively presented?*
- *Have I reflected on my observations of children playing the game?*
- *Can I adjust the game according to those observations?*

You may be asked to work with a group during the second half of the Literacy Hour, and this will vary according to the ability level and task. The following checklist may be helpful:

- Check that the children are clear about what is expected of them (usually they will just have been instructed by the teacher during the whole-class section although sometimes the teacher will have given you the task to explain). Ask them questions to check their knowledge and allow them to ask you questions.
- If necessary, demonstrate what has to be done.
- Once they have started, check them individually to see where further support is necessary.
- Praise specific points as they work (e.g. 'Well done, Darren. You have remembered to make the capital letters twice as tall!').
- Stop every now and then to give feedback and further instruction where needed.
- Remember that struggling readers in particular need a lot of encouragement.

Reading across the curriculum

Many of the reading development activities that take place in early years settings are discrete. In other words, they are specifically about language and literacy. However, there are also opportunities for reading to be developed in other subject areas. Here are some examples in order to develop your thinking about how you can extend children's reading skills in all areas of the curriculum.

Maths	matching shapes
	sorting and counting letters
Science	labels on displays
	talk about photographs
History	look at old books
	use of non-fiction books
Geography	directionality
	catalogues of home furnishings
Art	directionality
	shape and letter patterns
Technology	pop-up books
	puppets
Movement	characters from books
	journeys and explorations from books
Music	rhythm and rhyme
	sounds and listening games
ICT	reading game instructions
	word processing
Media	newspapers and magazines
	television texts
RE	religious books and stories
	stories from other cultures

Clearly, it is the teacher's responsibility to plan for these areas. However, it is important to remember that informed support for reading across the curriculum can make a real contribution to the continued development of children's reading. The discussion, explaining, comparing, repeating and matching that might take place with a story book are just as valid and as fruitful with non-fiction texts. It is also worth remembering to read aloud extracts from non-fiction for discussion as well as fiction.

Reading and play

When children are playing they can be exploring, learning, practising and extending a whole range of skills and concepts. The quality of the learning that takes place during play can depend very much on the provision of support. The support comes in the form of play materials and resources, but also in the form of adult intervention. We have already considered how resources might be provided, particularly in role play corners, to invite children to read. Let us now focus on your interventions by reflecting on several questions about your own practice.

- Do you ever go into role to join the child's fantasy?
- How do you draw attention to print?
- How do you model yourself as a reader?
- How do you respond if the child 'pretend' reads?
- How do you respond if the child just 'reads' the illustrations?
- What sorts of questions do you ask children when they are playing?
- Why is it sometimes better to observe from a distance?
- Do you sometimes provide additional playthings to cater for unexpected developments?
- How do you show the children that play is a worthwhile activity?
- How do you extend the play ideas into other activities?

Role play areas provide wonderful opportunities for children to extend their understanding of reading through play. It is very easy to collect a whole range of cost-free materials from all kinds of places to use for this purpose. For example:

- Shops
- Garages
- Transport depot
- Tourist information centres
- Hotels
- Restaurants
- Used magazines and newspapers

can provide a rich source of

- Leaflets
- Brochures
- Catalogues
- Posters
- Display materials
- Window dressing materials
- Scrap paper
- Carrier bags
- Bills
- Receipts
- Order pads
- Empty packaging

- Advertisements
- Boxes

- Food labels.

These resources can be used in many ways to encourage the children to play, read and explore texts.

Not only can these resources be used to create a bright and stimulating role play environment, they can also be used as resources for actual learning activities involving play. Mail-order catalogues, for instance, can really motivate children to use an index. Using laundry liquid bottles for measuring liquids can also provide opportunities to look at phonemes and words on the labels.

Supporting struggling readers in Year 3

Assistants are often asked to work with the least able children. The ALS, described in Chapter 2, targets children who are behind with reading and writing in Years 3 and 4 and is designed for implementation by assistants. Likewise, *The Catch Up Programme* (Bentley *et al.* 1999) targets Level 1 readers in Year 3, parts of which are delivered by support staff under the supervision of the teacher or special educational needs coordinator (SENCO).

Year 3 children are particularly vulnerable. They know they are behind their peers and have often become rather disillusioned with the reading process. The Key Stage 2 curriculum depends much more on literacy skills than in Key Stage 1 which means that these children can have problems in other subject areas as well. If they are not targeted for additional help at this point they can often fall further behind.

Clearly, you will be guided by the teachers with whom you are working. However, there are clear principles that will help you when you work with Year 3 strugglers:

- Praise and encouragement. This doesn't just help them to feel happier, it can also be an effective way of reinforcing their learning! 'Well done. You remembered the sound that c and h make when they are together. What was that sound again?'
- Bite-sized chunks. Too much too soon can be overwhelming for these children. Give them challenges that are within realistic reach while also moving them on a step. This allows success and a sense of achievement. Slow progress is better than refusal or reluctance due to fear of failure.
- Build on what they already know. Hopefully, your tasks will be based on diagnostic assessment of what they need to learn next. Teaching children what they already know or something too far advanced is wasting their time and yours.
- Make time for revision. If you work with children such as these on a regular basis, always recap on the previous session before starting something new. These children often need repetition and revision.
- Talk about reading. Very often, these children have a fixed idea that reading is just about fiction. Help them to broaden their understanding by showing them and talking about other texts, e.g. comics, food packets, TV guides, football programmes, etc.

Support is ongoing

Many of the situations and activities described in this chapter will already have been familiar to you. Working with individuals or small groups to help their reading is perhaps the most common area of support for assistants to provide. However, this chapter has also aimed to highlight that almost every minute of the day provides excellent opportunities for developing children's reading in a wide variety of ways. These are additional to the planned discrete teaching of reading activities. Labels on coat hooks and drawers, writing on displays, lists of words relating to topics, weather charts, registers, names and titles on workbooks and so on all provide ongoing opportunities for children to use and explore print. Drawing attention to texts, phoneme and word recognition, reading for a purpose, booktalk and the sheer pleasure of stories and books all help to develop young children's reading strategies, while at the same time giving them the implicit message that we regard them already as readers, that we respect their expertise and that we are firmly committed to extending that learning and development at every possible opportunity.

Notes for group leaders

⇨ Extend Activity 6.1 into a discussion in pairs taking turns to think of examples.

⇨ Display the games from Activity 6.3 for the whole group to see. Evaluate each other's games in pairs and give feedback.

⇨ Discuss the issues listed within the four categories of support.

⇨ In groups of six discuss experiences of hearing children read. Who? When? How long? How often? Recording? Individual differences and so on.

⇨ In groups of three look at a picture book then brainstorm follow-up activities across the curriculum.

⇨ In groups of four, brainstorm ideas for different role play corners and reading resources which could be provided for each.

Further reading

Baddeley, P. and Eddershaw, C. (1994) *Not So Simple Picture Books*. Stoke-on-Trent: Trentham Books.

Bentley, D. and Reid, D. (1995) *Supporting Struggling Readers*. Royston: United Kingdom Reading Association.

Bentley, D. *et al.* (1999) *The Catch Up Programme. Updated Edition*. See website: www.thecatchupproject.org

DfEE (1999) *The National Literacy Strategy: Additional Literacy Support*. London: DfEE.

Doonan, J. (1993) *Looking at Pictures in Picture Books*. Stroud: Thimble Press.

7 The developing writer

This chapter discusses the developmental nature of writing and how the experiences in early years settings (Figure 7.1) can build usefully upon the early learning that has already taken place at home. It examines the processes of writing, the early learning goals, National Curriculum levels and supporting children's writing in the Literacy Hour.

Figure 7.1 Writing can take place in a variety of media

How does writing develop?

Throughout this book, reference has been made to the importance of enabling children to engage in language activities where oracy, reading and writing are integrated. Much of what has been said in the discrete chapters on oracy and reading applies also to writing. By the time children start playgroup, nursery or school they have already accumulated a wealth of knowledge and understanding of the ways that language works. They will be familiar with print within the social environment, and most will have had considerable experience of stories and books. In addition they will have experimented with writing and probably regard themselves as writers within their own world of play.

Basic concepts acquired are likely to include:

- print carries meaning
- print is different from pictures
- the words we say can be encoded into print
- print can be spoken out loud
- print written in English moves across the page from left to right
- print is composed of different units – letters, words, spaces, sentences, etc.
- print comes in different shapes, colours and sizes
- writing is a meaningful activity
- adults write for many reasons
- adults read what other adults write.

These concepts are so basic to experienced writers that adults can sometimes undervalue them when accounting for what young children actually know, even though the concepts are built on significant experiences of texts. However, if such concepts are to be utilised as foundations for the development of future learning the momentum and motivation of this preschool writing should be maintained. Unfortunately, children can have quite misguided ideas about school 'work' and the expectations of teachers. It is quite common for children who are confident 'writers' at home and in nursery to become suddenly reluctant to write at school because they are afraid they might get it wrong. The links between the foundation stage and the National Curriculum now provide a developmental framework with clear guidelines for practitioners. However, it is vital for those who work with 5- to 8-year-olds to sustain the rich and interactive literacy environment provided by nurseries and reception classes so that children are learning through age appropriate activities that are meaningful and enjoyable. The tendency to over-formalise literacy learning at Key Stage 1 does not necessarily produce better results and can be disconcerting and discouraging to young children.

While recognising that children already have some foundation competencies in writing when they start school, we must also acknowledge that children will be at different stages of writing development. Some will write fluently and confidently, some will write their own name, some will be unable to distinguish numbers from letters and so on. The first vital thing that adults working with young children need to understand is the developmental framework within which writing grows and changes. Approaches to writing that take this into account provide *continuity* for the child rather than presenting the child with a new and strange set of experiences that could undermine his or her confidence in learning.

There have been various useful models to demonstrate the stages of development in children's writing. Marie Clay (1975), through her careful and systematic observations of children's early writing, identified certain features which appear to be common to very young children (Figures 7.2–7.6).

As with all developmental models, it is important not to regard such stages as independent units. There will always be overlap between phases as one merges into the other. However, what such models of developmental writing do help us with is the understanding that writing progresses – it changes. And those changes take place in a recognisable and sequential order. Recognition of the sequence enables us to define what the child has already learned and where he or she should be moving to next.

Figure 7.2 The recurring principle – repeated movements, e.g. loops

Figure 7.3 The generative principle – small number of letters repeated in different combinations

Figure 7.4 The sign concept – representational drawing, awareness that print carries message, e.g. McDonalds

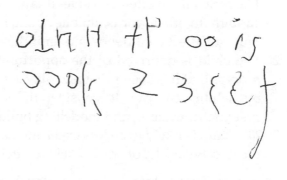

Figure 7.5 The flexibility principle – invention of letters, knowledge of similarities between letters leads to experimentation

Figure 7.6 Line and page principles – directionality, left–right, top–bottom, spaces between words, words as separate units

In Chapter 5, we looked at a model of reading in which the child moves from a supported role into independence. That same model is sometimes applied to writing, and is known as a 'developmental writing model'. The stages of ➡ **emergent** ➡ **supported** ➡ **fluent** ➡ **independent** have been one useful way of regarding the developmental flow of writing, and the recognition of the early concepts mentioned at the beginning of this chapter are encompassed within the term 'emergent writer'. Children's perceptions of themselves as writers play an important role in their motivation and confidence to learn. To feel that they have no skills to offer can be extremely discouraging when they suddenly find themselves in a new and strange environment.

One of the flaws in the particular developmental model is that it fails to acknowledge that children can be very independent in their early writing. Indeed, it could be argued that certain forms of support, for example teachers' writing for children to copy, actually presents a barrier to children's learning and slows down the impetus. Insisting that the child should copy an adult's version of what the child wants to say has three main drawbacks:

1. The child all too often perceives this as a message that his or her writing is not good enough. In other words, that he or she is no longer regarded by others as a writer. This can affect confidence and limit the child's motivation to write independently.
2. The child is deprived of the opportunity to sound out and invent spellings – a process that has been proven to play a valuable part in early spelling development by helping children to consider the sounds within the parts of words. (More systematic teaching and modelling builds on this conceptual awareness later.)
3. The child is likely to be less experimental in the things he or she plans to write and the vocabulary he or she is likely to attempt.

It is therefore helpful to use a developmental framework that recognises and empowers the child as an independent writer from the beginning and identifies the progressive features that should emerge as the child's writing develops. One example of such a model is presented below (Clipson-Boyles 1996).

☐ *The emergent writer* understands the function of print and writes for different purposes in his or her play. This writing cannot normally be decoded by a reader who has not observed the process and listened to the child's accompanying talk.

☐ *The exploratory writer* actively relates sounds to meaning through his or her own invented spellings. This writer is confident in his or her own ideas, perceives him- or herself as a writer and does not copy-write from an adult's writing above his or her own.

☐ *The communicative writer* writes texts which can be read by others. This writer seeks out, independently, letter and sound information from a range of sources, e.g. books, adults, other children, posters, word cards, displays. He or she will sometimes change words after they have been written.

☐ *The reflective writer* checks, reconsiders and redrafts his or her work. This redrafting is based on a recognition of the need for accuracy in punctuation, spelling and grammar. He or she is able to discuss his or her writing retrospectively and evaluates the effectiveness of his or her communication.

☐ *The versatile writer* is able to plan and adapt his or her style according to the purpose of and audience for the writing, and is able to move text around in order to reorganise his or her ideas when necessary. The majority of the writing is produced correctly, but ambitious use of extended vocabulary means that more challenging words are sometimes misspelt. Editing and redrafting will take place in order to develop the quality of the work even further.

Developmental stages of the early years independent writer

ACTIVITY 7.1 – Time: 30 minutes

With the permission of the teacher, make a collection of photocopies of children's writing and try to match the stages of development with one or more of the models discussed so far. For the Clipson-Boyles model you will also need to observe the children at work to check on the processes taking place at the time of writing.

A framework for teaching

Allowing children to explore and experiment independently does not mean leaving them to their own devices in the hope that the learning will just happen! The foundation stage curriculum guidelines (DfEE and QCA 2000), National Curriculum (DfEE and QCA 1999a) and NLS (DfEE 1998) provide a structured framework for good practice with clear measurable targets for children's learning. These can be achieved through structured learning opportunities and the good models of teaching described in the previous chapter.

The early learning goals towards which children are working during the foundation stage are described as follows:

- Use phonic knowledge to write regular simple words and make phonetically plausible attempts at more complex words.
- Attempt writing for different purposes, using features of different forms such as lists, stories, instructions.
- Write their own names and other things such as labels and captions and begin to form simple sentences, sometimes using punctuation.
- Use a pencil and hold it effectively to form recognisable letters, most of which are correctly formed.

(DfEE and QCA 2000, p. 26)

The additional goal for linking sounds and letters overlaps between reading and writing as explained in Chapter 5. It is important to remember that these are the goals to aim for by the time children start in Year 1. The two years leading up to that time will be providing rich and exciting opportunities for children to develop these skills. For example, paint and sand play are helping children to develop directionality and motor control. See the curriculum guidelines for more examples (DfEE and QCA 2000).

Once the child begins school, they are working towards the National Curriculum Attainment Targets. These are described as follows:

Level 1: Pupils' writing communicates meaning through simple words and phrases. In their reading or their writing, pupils show an awareness of how full stops are used. Letters are usually clearly shaped and correctly orientated.

Level 2: Pupils' writing communicates meaning in both narrative and non-narrative forms, using appropriate interest and vocabulary, and showing some awareness of the reader. Ideas are developed in a sequence of sentences, sometimes demarcated by capital letters and full stops. Simple, monosyllabic words are usually spelt correctly, and where there are inaccuracies the alternative is phonetically plausible. In handwriting, letters are accurately formed and consistent in size.

Level 3: Pupils' writing is often organised, imaginative and clear. The main features of different forms of writing are used appropriately, beginning to be adapted for different readers. Sequences of sentences extend ideas logically and words are chosen for variety and interest. The basic grammatical structure of sentences is usually correct. Spelling is usually accurate, including that of common polysyllabic words. Punctuation to mark sentences – full stops, capital letters and question marks – is used accurately. Handwriting is joined and legible.

(DfEE and QCA 1999a, p. 58)

The NLS (DfEE 1998) provides a structured syllabus of what should be taught in which term and it is recommended that you familiarise yourself with this framework so that you understand why teachers are planning their Literacy Hour in the ways that they do. However, it is equally essential for you to understand the core processes of writing.

The processes of writing

Imagine that you are looking at two stories written by seven-year-olds. One is in neatly joined handwriting, complete with full stops, capital letters and mostly correct spellings. The other is scrawled and untidy with evidence of many misspelt words. Your first impression might be that the first child is a 'better writer' than the second. Then, upon closer inspection, you note the following features:

- *Story 1* – short simple sentences, limited vocabulary, little description, muddled tenses, unclear storyline.
- *Story 2* – complex sentences with good use of conjunctions, misspelt words are nevertheless phonologically systematic and are ambitious/adventurous vocabulary, storyline is well developed with good description of characters, mood and action.

How do we begin to assess which is the better piece of writing? The answer is that we can't make a general comparison between the two. We need to separate out the different components of the writing in order to see how each child is progressing within the different skill areas. Child 1 has a well developed style of handwriting, fluent, legible and presentable, but needs more work on sentence construction and use of vocabulary. Child 2 is a skilled story writer and an accomplished sculptor of words, but needs to develop more control over her handwriting. This hypothetical example is intended to illustrate the fact that when supporting children in their writing we need to be aware of the different processes that are involved.

Frank Smith (1982) divided these components into two groups called 'authorship skills' and 'secretarial skills'. Authorship skills are about style, organisation, communication, development of ideas, creativity, adaptability to audience and purpose and sensitivity to the audience. Secretarial skills include spelling, punctuation, grammar and presentation.

The art of the supporting adult is to know when it is appropriate to intervene and why. Table 7.1 illustrates how it can be appropriate to offer certain types of support at different stages of the writing process.

Table 7.1 Stages of adult support during writing processes

Adult support for secretarial	Child's writing processes	Adult support for authorship
	Planning	◄— Stimulus provision
		◄— Encouraging discussion
	First draft	◄— Encourage independence
Suggest focus for checks (e.g. full stops) —►	Checking back	◄— Respond to meaning
		◄— Ask questions
		◄— Read together
Child checks spellings with support —►	Redrafting	◄— Encourage independence
Reads aloud for accuracy —►	Correcting	
Evaluates presentation —►		
Revise handwriting rules —►	Final draft	◄— Reminder of purpose
Reminder of reader's needs —►		

Supporting children's spelling

Adults can sometimes have very unreasonable expectations of children's spellings – and their frustration shows when they try to correct a large percentage of a child's writing. Not only is this very discouraging to the child, it is also unrealistic to expect a child to digest such a vast amount of input in one go. Far better to prioritise fewer words, choosing those which the child will learn most easily. One way of tuning in to where children are at with their spelling is to relate it to a developmental framework for spelling.

Gentry (1987) proposes that children's spelling moves through five identifiable stages:

1. *Precommunicative stage* where the child writes down random shapes and letters and numbers to represent meaning. This is unlikely to be legible to another reader.
2. *Semiphonetic stage* where the child represents whole chunks of sounds with single letters, e.g. fm = farm, tct = tractor.

3. *Phonetic stage* where the child introduces vowels and represents most of the sounds phonetically, e.g. camru = camera, sestu = sister.
4. *Transitional stage* where the child starts to demonstrate a knowledge of spelling patterns and rules, e.g. trolly = trolley, powny = pony.
5. *Correct stage* where the child has a good understanding of spelling rules, can apply these to attempts at new words, and visualise and say spellings before writing them down.

This model is particularly helpful when assessing children's writing because it provides a clear diagnostic framework for teachers when they are planning a spelling programme. It also helps adults to decipher what children are writing and understand the level of their approach.

Spelling involves a complex set of brain processes. These include what we see, what we hear, what we remember and how we feel the directional movement of our pen. It is therefore appropriate that spelling is taught with these multi-sensory skills in mind, and teachers usually employ a range of methods to help children to develop their spelling vocabulary.

Adults who are assisting children in their writing need to consider the following when providing additional support for spelling.

- Respect children's own attempts.
- Clap the rhythms of the words to identify the syllables.
- Play and have fun with words and sounds.
- Note any patterns in their mistakes and prioritise what they need to learn next.
- Always encourage the children to have a go first before writing a word for them.
- Help the children to say the sounds aloud and think about the order of those sounds.
- Draw on the children's existing alphabet knowledge.
- Draw attention to the parts of words (chunks).
- Encourage the use of memory (look and cover).
- Practise the 'feel' of letter groups (linking with handwriting).
- Link writing to reading.
- Write three versions of a word for children to choose the correct version.
- Make links with other similar words.
- Discourage dictionaries at the first draft stage.
- Encourage dictionaries at the redraft stage.
- Let the children highlight words which need correcting – they usually do know.
- Explain that spotting mistakes isn't a sign of failure, it is a sign of success.
- Let the children see you using a dictionary sometimes – we all need them!

Handwriting

Handwriting should be taught correctly from an early stage and schools will have a clearly defined handwriting policy. Habits, once formed, are very hard to change, so getting it right from the start is important. Supporting adults should ensure that they are familiar with the nursery or school policy so that they are modelling the correct approach to letter formation and strokes. Handwriting is a motor skill that has to be taught and practised. It is such a physical part of the writing process that individual checking and support is usually needed. The following checklist is designed to help you with this task:

- Is the child sitting comfortably?
- Can the child see his or her paper?
- How is the child holding his or her pencil?
- Is the child leaving spaces between words?
- Is the child recognising the heights of tall and upper case letters?
- Are the letter formations in line with the school policy?

In addition, if the child is left-handed:

- Does the child have enough elbow room?
- Are they sitting to the left of his or her neighbour?
- Is the paper to the child's left, tilted slightly so he or she can see child writing?
- Are you demonstrating in a way that is possible with the left hand?
- Are you allowing the child enough time?

ACTIVITY 7.2 – Time: 5 minutes

Using Activity Sheet 13 'Handwriting', make a copy of the text using the hand that you don't normally use for writing.

Figure 7.7 Play provides valuable contexts for writing

Writing and play

Writing activities can have a very appropriate place within children's play activities, particularly if they represent a natural progression to the play as chosen by the child (Figure 7.7). Within a play context the child is usually in charge of the decision-making and therefore the writing is driven by the child's motivation or need to write. However, the likelihood of the child making that choice is also dependent upon the resources available. If there is a message pad and pen by the telephone in the home corner he or she is far more likely to write a 'message' than if there is not. Many nurseries have a writing corner, where children can use the resources to write for any purpose they have identified – this might spring from other areas of play (e.g. making a bill for the car the child has just repaired) or might be a discrete writing activity (e.g. writing a story). Such writing corners work well where there is a variety of resources such as:

- different shapes of paper
- different coloured paper
- different sizes of paper
- scrap paper and best paper
- lined paper and plain paper
- envelopes
- bookmaking resources
- folders
- range of writing implements (including pens)
- pencil sharpeners
- rubbers
- stencils
- hole punchers
- labels
- typewriters
- post box
- words on display
- examples of texts
- dictionaries and thesauruses.

Children should have free access to these resources but should also be taught how to use them correctly and leave the area tidy. Modelling the writing process by taking part in the role play can help you to structure children's play into more purposeful learning activities. The questions you ask and references you make to other things will all help to support and extend children's writing.

ACTIVITY 7.3 – Time: 15 minutes

Make a list of the types of writing opportunities that could be provided in four different role play corners. Consider the types of intervention you could make to extend the children's skills and knowledge of writing.

ICT

Writing at the computer offers children excellent opportunities to link reading and writing (Figure 7.8). It also encourages children to edit easily, and produce a presentable piece of text. All children should be taught computer skills from an early age if they are to be prepared for the technological society in which we now live. When supporting children at the computer try to encourage them to:

- use all their fingers for typing
- use their thumbs for the space bar
- write first then edit
- print out and highlight corrections
- read back their own work
- store their work and come back to it later where appropriate.

Figure 7.8 Computers provide valuable reading and writing opportunities for young children

Writing across the curriculum

There are reasons for children to write in most areas of the curriculum (Table 7.2). This variety offers children the opportunity to write in different ways and for different purposes. Children are much more motivated to write when:

- they have a good reason for writing
- there is an interested audience waiting for their writing
- they have something to write about
- the writing is likely to illicit a response or reply
- they have resources to stimulate their writing
- they feel safe to experiment.

Table 7.2 Types of writing across the curriculum

Activity	Curriculum area	Format
Collect and draw mini-beasts	Science	Chart
Word games	Literature	Lists
Seasons word play	Science	Word collages
		List poems
		Shape poems
Clothes lists	Science	List
Weather recording	Geography/science	Diary
Bookmaking	Various	Books
Sequencing and writing	Various	Story
Cooking	Technology	Recipe card
Model-making	Technology	Plan or list
Diagrams	Various	Labels
Messages to . . .	Language	Letters
Puppet plays	Language	Story scripts
Greetings cards	Language/RE	Card
Write to people in hospital	Topic	Letter
Instructions for a game	Various	Ordered list
Word trees	Various	One word per leaf
Recycling sorting	Science	Chart
Advertising/appeals	Various	Posters
Papermaking	Technology	Reporting
Class newspaper	Language	Ads, news, class
Joke book	Language	Page layout
Role play corner	Language/topic	Various
Sorting	Maths	Recording
Shape	Maths	Description

Many of these activities will be familiar to you and you will no doubt know many more. The National Curriculum stresses the importance of this sort of *range* in children's writing. They should have opportunities to write in different ways for different reasons and for a variety of audiences. This includes writing in different formats and also in different styles. Confidence, fluency and accuracy are listed as key skills, and pupils should also be given opportunities to plan and review their writing. Punctuation, spelling and handwriting are each outlined in particular as are Standard English and knowledge about language.

ACTIVITY 7.4 – Time: 20 minutes

On a piece of paper, make a list of the different purposes, audiences and forms for writing which you have observed in the settings where you work. Which do you notice the children enjoying the most? Why?

Making links between writing, reading and talk

Texts provide models for children's writing. The discussions you have with children when they are reading, about words, spaces, letters, full stops and so on are actively feeding in to their writing (Figure 7.9). Drawing attention to features in books and other texts is an important skill of the supporting adult. Every contact with a text is an opportunity to learn about writing.

When children are attempting their own spellings, saying and listening are crucial parts of the process. Sounding out the phonemes, having fun with rhymes and distinguishing between the beginnings and endings of words are all helping to reinforce word construction skills.

Figure 7.9 Supporting children through discussing their writing

Collaborative writing

Collaborative writing is not just about writing in groups or pairs. It is also about the nature of the writing process. It is about not writing in isolation, but taking opportunities to consult in a range of ways.

The collaborative writer might consult:

pupils
teachers
parents
other adults
editors
books

in order to obtain:
feedback
advice
information
ideas
comment
other resources
previous work
dictionaries
thesauruses
other texts

This collaboration enhances the learning benefits of the overall process. Supporting adults can be there for consultation, but should also be aware of these other places where the children should be encouraged to seek out what they need. Actively encouraging children to make their own decisions about such collaboration makes an important contribution to children's developing thinking, confidence and independence.

Responding to children's writing

The ways in which you respond to children's writing will play an important part in what they attempt next. Nurseries and schools will have different approaches to the ways in which children's work is corrected, but for those who play a supporting role, the following guidelines provide a framework for response that is designed to encourage and extend learning.

- Respond to the content first.
- Show an interest in the writing.
- Ask the child about the subject matter.
- Ask the child what he or she thinks of the writing.
- Read the writing together.
- Praise the attempts at spellings before pointing out they are wrong.
- Do not overload the child with too many mistakes to think about (i.e. consider what is most appropriate for the child to learn next).
- Ask if the child would like to change or check anything.

Where possible, it is useful to write a response to the child. This enables the writing and reading to interlink in a very meaningful way but also enables you to model the spellings which the child has not yet learned. Figure 7.10 demonstrates how the adult has responded to the child's writing by showing interest, asking a question and also modelling some of the words which the child misspelt.

Giving children encouragement is not just designed to keep them happy. It is a way of ensuring that they will want to try again rather than feeling they have failed or are not capable of the task in hand. Encouragement can be given for:

- having a go
- using interesting words
- changing and correcting own writing
- checking a word

Figure 7.10 Responding and modelling

ACTIVITY 7.5 – Time: ongoing

Use Activity Sheet 14 'Reflecting on your own practices' to focus on aspects of your own practice. Do not overload yourself with too many questions at once! Wherever possible, discuss these with the teacher and where necessary list some action points on the back of the sheet. Plan to revisit these at a later date to monitor your progress.

- experimenting with new ideas
- taking the initiative
- reflecting on their own writing.

Notes for group leaders

⇨ Ask the students to bring in the samples collected for Activity 7.1 and compare them. Discuss the features and stages of development and what certain children might need to learn next in terms of their writing.

⇨ Discuss Activity 7.2 to see how it felt. What are the implications for where the paper is positioned when two children are writing together?

⇨ As an extension of Activity 7.3, in pairs, plan and make writing resources for a role play corner.

⇨ Have a group discussion about the writing policies known to the group.

⇨ Asking the group to work as individuals set them a writing task under limited time conditions and with little or no stimulus or discussion. At the end, ask how they felt while writing, what else would they have liked to know, what would they like to happen to their writing next, etc.

⇨ Share experiences of how to support children's writing in the Literacy Hour.

Further reading

Alston, J. (1995) *Assessing and Promoting Writing Skills*. Stafford: NASEN.

Browne, A. (1999) *Teaching Writing at Key Stage 1 and Before*. London: Nelson Thornes.

Hall, N. and Robinson, A. (1995) *Exploring Writing and Play in the Early Years*. London: David Fulton Publishers.

Hodson, P. and Jones, D. (2001) *Teaching Children to Write*. London: David Fulton Publishers.

Redfern, A. (1993) *Practical Ways to Teach Spelling*. Reading: Reading and Language Information Centre.

Taylor, J. (2001) *Handwriting: A Teacher's Guide*. London: David Fulton Publishers.

8 Supporting second language learners

Many children in the UK are learning English as an Additional Language (EAL). Sadly, this was sometimes regarded as an additional responsibility by some schools who were so used to the monolingual culture that was a feature of living on an island. Yet in other developed countries of the world bilingualism and multilingualism are the norm. Indeed in some countries it is considered to be a considerable social disadvantage to speak, read and write only one language.

The language and literacy frameworks presented in this book provide good models of practice for supporting second language learners. However, this chapter sets out to discuss some of the particular issues relating to bilingualism and biliteracy, and looks at some of the practical implications of providing effective support for, and enhancement of, a range of languages, including English, in early years settings.

Building good foundations

It is difficult, if not impossible, to separate out multilingual issues from the political and social agendas of our time. While it is not the main purpose of this chapter to discuss multiculturalism, anti-racism and equal opportunities in great depth, it is important nevertheless to point out that the successful and healthy development of these areas are dependent on everything we do in early years settings.

The ways in which adults approach language and literacy in early years settings are ingrained with attitudes and implied messages. If we are to succeed in our mission to help children develop the necessary language skills we must develop a sound understanding and awareness of the fact that all we do and say has an impact upon the children in our care. Bearing that in mind, there are three basic truths that should be central to our practice.

1. The linguistic needs of EAL learners require both languages to be respected, valued and used in their learning

Research (Cummins 1994) and projects (e.g. Multilingual Resources for Children Project 1995) have demonstrated that helping children to be confident in their own language gives them a firmer foundation upon which to build the learning of their second language. In other words there are sound linguistic reasons for not excluding the home language from the educational setting.

2. The social and psychological needs of EAL learners require both languages to be respected, valued and used in their learning

Our language is part of our identity. To prevent or discourage children from using their home and community language can undermine their confidence and self-esteem. It is also giving an insidious message of the superiority of English over their own language. Tension between the two languages can lead to conflict and confusion. Alternatively, to demonstrate to children that their language is valued and respected can provide a positive approach to learning the two languages side by side.

3. The linguistic, social and psychological needs of monolingual English speakers require a variety of languages to be respected, valued and used in their learning

The Cox Report (DES 1988) recommended that one of the ways children should learn language is through learning *about* language. This is referred to now as KAL (Knowledge About Language). Exploring the diversity of languages, accents and dialects, including Standard English, can help children to develop their knowledge and understanding of how language works, and is required by the National Curriculum and NLS. The multilingual setting offers a rich resource for learning not only about languages and texts, but also about how to build mutually rewarding relationships between children from different cultural backgrounds. Such learning is important for all monolingual English-speaking children, regardless of the cultural mix in their community.

ACTIVITY 8.1 – Time: ongoing

Before embarking upon this activity you will need to consult with your teacher mentor and your head teacher or whoever is in charge of your workplace. Using a copy of Activity Sheet 15 'Recording children's knowledge of languages in addition to English', make a careful record of the language knowledge of eight children. If there are no EAL children available to you it will still be interesting to see what awareness and knowledge young monolinguals have of other languages.

Knowledge of languages

All adults working with young children have a responsibility to acquire a certain knowledge of the languages and backgrounds of those children. This does not mean becoming fluent in all the languages you are likely to encounter! That would be unrealistic. But to learn a few simple words, particularly greetings, gives a strong message that you are not only interested, but also approving and accepting. Involving the child in teaching you (and the other children) more about his or her language is also a valuable way into discussion about language skills.

Other information you might need to obtain includes:

- Do both parents speak the same language?
- Is the home language also a community language?

- Is the spoken language the same as the written?
- In which direction does the written text travel?
- Is there a special language for the purposes of religion?
- Is the child educated by other educators (e.g. community language teachers)?

It is also helpful to understand common terminology relating to additional language issues. The following words are often used to talk about language.

accent	– variation in pronunciation
dialect	– variations in grammatical structure/vocabulary
monolingual	– speaks in one language proficiently
bilingual	– regularly uses two languages to speak
biliterate	– able to read and write in two languages
multilingual	– speaks three or more languages (not necessarily proficient)
TEFL	– Teaching English as a Foreign Language
ESL	– English as a Second Language
EAL	– English as an Additional Language
TESOL	– Teaching English to Speakers of Other Languages

In this chapter, the term 'multilingual setting' is used to refer to a place where there are three or more languages, including English, spoken by different children.

ACTIVITY 8.2 – Time: 90 minutes

Go to your local library and find out which are the most common languages spoken in your area using council information. Then, using books from the library make a copy of the words 'Welcome' or 'Hello' in as many different scripts as you can find. Ask the librarians where else you can go to find out more about particular languages that are spoken in your area.

Figure 8.1 Sharing dual language books offers a rich source of discussion and interest

Why do EAL children need additional support?

Language exists in order for us to communicate. We cannot communicate alone! Throughout this book, the integrated nature of language has been discussed. The links between speaking, listening, reading and writing are a natural and constructive part of children's language learning. These processes are interactive and require exchanges with others. EAL children benefit enormously from working in English-speaking groups because it gives them opportunities to:

- listen to the sounds of English
- observe the exchanges of others
- practise responding in English
- ask questions
- answer questions
- repeat what they hear
- use body language for clues
- receive support from other children.

Working in a pair with a child who speaks the same home language offers EAL children opportunities to:

- consolidate ideas
- clarify areas of uncertainty
- answer questions
- translate
- develop confidence in their learning.

Working in a pair with a child who speaks English (Figure 8.1) offers both children opportunities to:

- write dual texts
- discuss and translate
- listen to both languages
- speak both languages
- teach each other about their languages.

Working with an English-speaking supporting adult offers EAL children opportunities to:

- share their worries
- ask questions in English
- answer questions in English
- repeat and practise
- revisit previous learning
- talk about their home language
- 'teach' the adult
- enjoy looking at books
- observe writing.

Working with a supporting adult who speaks the child's home language (Figure 8.2) offers that child opportunities to do all the things in the previous list plus:

- develop their home language
- learn to switch between languages
- listen to ideas explained in their own language
- have instructions translated
- answer questions in their own language
- ask questions in their own language; and
- conceptualise ideas in their own language.

Working on their own, EAL children have no opportunity to experiment, listen and respond. Isolated and passive learning situations are totally inappropriate to their needs for dynamic interaction.

Figure 8.2 Support should be offered in the home language as well as English

---

ACTIVITY 8.3 – Time: 30 minutes

Using Activity Sheet 16 'Bilingual group observations', make a record of your observations of EAL children working in groups. (If you do not have the opportunity to observe EAL children in your own workplace, it would be well worth making your own arrangements to visit another setting.) Explain and discuss your task with those who are in charge so that they can agree to the activity and perhaps even offer you advice about which children to observe. The sheet describes the observation process in more detail.

Examples of interactive activities

The interactive contexts mentioned above can operate right across the curriculum. Activities that are particularly useful to language learners are:

Bookmaking   Storytelling and technology create an active learning situation in which children can talk, listen, write, read, make and draw.

Booktalk   Sharing picture books enables the EAL child to listen, say and look. The pictures provide a strong context for the child to make meaning. Books with a cumulative repeated pattern are also useful for enjoyable practice, as are rhyming and rhythmic verse. Books which have a box of related artefacts are particularly useful. Making storyboxes can also be fun for the children.

Storytelling	Telling known stories, new stories or stories about oneself – the ancient art of storytelling is central to human existence and is a completely cross-cultural activity, as natural as talk itself!
Retelling	Right across the curriculum, the opportunity to retell reaps rich rewards for EAL learners. Artefacts can serve a useful purpose in reminding the child as he or she retells. These could range from the seeds which have just been planted, to the clothes to be put on after PE.
Drama/Role play	Playing the roles of others help children to explore and experiment with a range of language for a variety of purposes.
Puppets	Designing and making puppets is fun, but to use them is even better. Links with storymaking and technology again make this a dynamic hands-on activity with a lot of purposeful communication.
Masks	A mask can help to give a child the confidence to speak because he or she has a shield. The child can also become someone else. Characters from stories can be a powerful voice for a child to use when developing confidence in spoken language.
Photographs	Photographs of the children, their families and other related subjects can be a tremendously stimulating resource for young children. They can be used for discussion, displays, art activities and bookmaking.
Cooking	Nothing motivates children quite like cooking, except perhaps eating! Cooking provides particularly good opportunities to explore cultural variety in an exciting and experiential way.
Visitors	A visitor is a focus for attention, whether that visitor is a newborn baby or the local vet. Listening and questioning have a real context when appropriate people visit an early years setting, and the activity provides an opportunity to broaden the variety of role models for the children.
Visits	Educational visits do not have to take all day and needn't cost anything. The local area will always provide a good range of resources to stimulate children's language, and provide excellent starting points for learning by building on what the children know well.
Festivals	Festivals provide a starting point for a wide range of cross-curricular and discrete language development work. These should be explored meaningfully rather than through token reference.
Play	All play activities provide opportunities for language development. The talk which takes place during play can be an important mechanism for allowing children to organise their thoughts. Toys give children additional cues for their spoken language.

Writing corners A writing area which is resourced with a wide range of writing implements, different types, sizes, colours and shapes of paper and displays of different types of texts can be very inviting to children if they are encouraged and rewarded for their efforts.

Listening corners Listening to story tapes with a book is a popular activity for all children. Tapes can also be used for games, instructions and repeating an activity. It is very rewarding for children to make their own tapes in addition to using commercial tapes.

Computers Programs with a high graphic input alongside the text are invaluable to EAL learners. Multimedia systems (though few schools can afford these at the moment) are of particular benefit as they also incorporate sound and therefore are completely interactive.

Dual language books

Dual language texts have been well received by teachers and pupils in Britain since the mid-1980s. They offer all children the opportunity to examine and learn about another language, while at the same time supporting children who are learning English as a second language (Figure 8.3). Indeed, dual language texts can be used in a variety of valuable ways.

However, they do vary so much in quality that it is important for adults in early years settings to develop a critical awareness of these books in order to enhance their use and, where appropriate, influence purchasing decisions. The following questions are designed to help you focus your attention on a dual language text in a way which critically evaluates the book.

- Which language comes first?
- Does one language have more prominence on the page?
- Are both languages written in the same size?
- Does each language have equal status?
- How has the inclusion of two texts affected the page layout?
- If one language is required to run in a different direction to English what effect does this have on the reader?
- How will the book be read?
- Are the pictures useful to the reader?
- Is the author English?
- Is the story from the culture of the home language?

Single language books

It is appropriate and educationally sound to provide children with texts written in their home language in addition to solely English texts and dual language texts. Not only does it help to build the sound foundations of language and literacy in the home

Figure 8.3 Dual language labels help EAL children but are also interesting to all children

language, it helps to develop and maintain a sense of cultural ownership of those stories. To deprive children of stories and authors from their own cultures is to deprive them of a valuable part of their developing sense of self and can also affect their language development.

Developing a supportive relationship

Many of the qualities that you already offer when supporting children's learning will be appropriate and helpful to EAL children when working with them through the day or more specifically during the Literacy Hour. The following general principles can be applied regardless of the activity you have been asked to support:

- Do not patronise. These children are language experts!
- Tune in to what the children know.
- Take an interest in their language.
- Take an interest in their culture.
- Ask them to teach you some words.
- Try to link sounds to images.
- Use artefacts when explaining.
- Draw when explaining.
- Use artefacts when reading and telling stories.
- Make good use of pictures when using books.
- Include pictures in all writing activities.
- Use lots of body language to enhance meaning.
- Repeat what you have said often.
- Ask the children to repeat what you have said often.
- Ask the children to retell what others (e.g. teacher) have said.
- Be a good listener.

- Learn from what you hear.
- Correct mistakes by being a role model rather than a critic.

Notes for group leaders

⇨ Sharing experiences through discussion will be particularly important for this topic as there is likely to be a wide range of views and experiences.

⇨ Wherever possible, Activities 8.1 and 8.3 should be planned and discussed with a mentor, or a training colleague.

⇨ Additional group activities could include:
  - puppet-making
  - collecting artefacts for a story
  - designing a role play corner
  - making dual language books
  - making books with photographs
  - making dual language labels and signs.

Further reading

Baker, C. (2000) *The Care and Education of Young Bilinguals*. Clevedon (UK): Multilingual Matters.

DES (1985) *Education For All*. (The Swann Report). London: HMSO.

Edwards, V. (1995) *Reading in Multilingual Classrooms*. Reading: Reading and Language Information Centre.

Edwards, V. (1995) *Speaking and Listening in Multilingual Classrooms*. Reading: Reading and Language Information Centre.

Edwards, V. (1995) *Writing in Multilingual Classrooms*. Reading: Reading and Language Information Centre.

Thompson, L. (1999) *Young Bilingual Learners in Nursery Schools*. Clevedon (UK): Multilingual Matters.

Activity sheets

The sheets on the following pages may be photocopied for use in activities and study. This includes the reproduction of more than one copy by purchasing institutions for educational purposes within that institution only.

Reflecting on yourself in working partnerships

Think about your main current working partnership. If you are not currently employed, try to recall a partnership from a previous post, or with a fellow trainee.

What qualities do you think you bring to this partnership?

What qualities does the other person bring to the partnership?

What is the worst problem you have encountered in this partnership?

How did you deal with this?

In retrospect, how would you like to deal with it differently if that was possible?

How do you usually respond to criticism from other people?

Think of an area of your work to criticise. Make a negative statement about it here as if it was being said by someone else!

Try to think of a creative response to the criticism, perhaps identifying three action points to follow.

Now try to find someone with whom you can discuss your responses to this activity. Decide first what you want to gain from the discussion.

Developing team skills

As you ask yourself the following questions make private notes for yourself. Other ways of developing your team skills may include:

- talking to others
- observing others
- setting yourself realistic goals
- writing down what you would like to aim for
- re-evaluating yourself in six months time

1. Belief system
- Am I committed to the overall success of the team?
- Do I expect my team leader to take all responsibility?
- Do I have high expectations of the team's work?

2. Self-awareness
- What are my own strengths and skills?
- What are my own limitations?
- What are the areas for development in my own practice?
- What is my role within the group?
- When should I ask for help and advice?

3. Social skills
- Do I support the needs of others?
- Am I a good listener?
- What impact do I have on others?
- Do I avoid problems?
- Am I committed to exploring conflict and resolving difficulties?
- Do I recognise the importance of honest relationships?
- Do I respect the feelings of others?
- Do I respect different viewpoints?
- Do I know when it is appropriate to speak up?
- Do I know when it is more useful to keep quiet?

4. Professional skills
- Do I take advice constructively?
- Do I give advice constructively?
- Do I communicate clearly?
- Do I work with and not against others?
- How do I think creatively?
- How do I demonstrate flexibility?
- How do I share the responsibility of decision-making?
- Am I clear about my role but not inflexible?
- Can I work independently without undermining the work of the team?
- Do I reflect and build continuously on my performance and practice?

Variety in language

Choose three of the language communities listed in Figure 2.2 in Chapter 2. In the three sections below list the differences between them by thinking about: (a) vocabulary and (b) purposes.

An example has been completed for you.

SITUATION: visit to the seaside

Vocabulary
sand, sea, bucket, spade,
seagull, hotel, visitors,
costumes, jet-ski, etc.

Purposes
asking about new experiences
asking for treats
describing new sights
describing emotions
'reading' attractions posters

SITUATION:

Vocabulary

Purposes

SITUATION:

Vocabulary

Purposes

SITUATION:

Vocabulary

Purposes

Play and language

Observation record

Child: _____ **Date:** _____

Activity: _____

Description of actions, spoken language and interactions with texts

Child observations

Child's name: _____

In a pair

Date: _____ Context: _____

In a small group (e.g. 3 or 4)

Date: _____ Context: _____

Whole-class situation (e.g. storytime)

Date: _____ Context: _____

One-to-one with an adult

Date: _____ Context: _____

Self-evaluation

Context: _____

Number of children: _____

How did I find out what they already knew?

How did I introduce the activity?

Did my questions encourage discussion or single answers?

How much opportunity did I give the children to ask questions?

How did I know what each child had learned by the end?

What might I do differently if I could repeat this activity?

Analysing your own talk

Think back to when you woke up yesterday and imagine that your day was recorded on video! In the first two columns below, record as much of the talk as you can remember by mentally recalling the order of events and the people to whom you spoke. It might help to do this chronologically.

Next, try to examine each example more closely by listing the *reason* for your talk and what sort of talk it was. Two examples have been given to guide you.

Situation	Person	Example	Type of talk
In bed	Son	Shouted to get him to turn his music down!	Command
Telephone	BT clerk	Complained about bill	Complaint questions

Thinking about your talk with children

The following questions are designed to help you to reflect on your own practice. Every day we talk automatically, sometimes without thinking about what we say and how we say it. A closer, critical examination of that talk can be useful and sometimes surprising.

- When starting a group activity do you give the pupils chance to talk about what they already know?

- When you explain something do you give the children chance to ask questions?

- When you give instructions how do you know they are clear?

- When you ask questions is there always only one answer?

- Do your questions open up possibilities for discussion?

- Do you allow the children to bring in their own ideas and experience where appropriate even if this takes you away from the original point?

- How do you show children that you are listening?

- How do you show children that you value their contributions?

- If a child offers a totally wrong answer how do you respond so that he or she does not feel embarrassed or discouraged?

- What is the balance between your talk and that of the pupils?

- How do you decide when pupil talk is off-task?

- What techniques do you use to move the talk back on-task?

- Is a reprimand always an effective way to do this?

- How can your attitude towards the children help to improve their listening skills?

- In a whole-class situation, how might you involve those pupils who are 'on the fringe'?

ACTION POINTS:

What do I do when I read?

On the chart below, make notes about how you read the different types of text listed.

Text	What do I do when I read this?
Magazine	
Telephone directory	
Recipe	
Newspaper	
Junk mail	
Party political leaflets	
Personal letter	
News item with difficult and unusual foreign names	
TV guide	
Special offers	

Analysing your reading strategies

> Below you will find four unusual examples of text. Cover these up immediately without looking at them. One at a time, uncover the texts and try to read them. Make notes after each one of the strategies you have used to decipher and understand what is written.

Text 1

The fat cat was too large to squeeze through the cat flap.

Text 2

Lxst wxxk I vxsxtxed my mxthxr xnd fxthxr. I dxdnt knxw thxt my sxstxr wxs xlsx gxxng tx bx thxrx. Wx hxd x gxxd chxt bxcxxsx wx hxdnt sxxn xxch xthxr fxr x lxng txmx.

Text 3

viss iss u spilink lisst ken u reid ve wudz buk knighs trea soopa pownd phinnish throo seeling benniffitt skweez schoopeed owver reesint bredd

Text 4

Little Rid Reding Hood was unsure about which path she should take. The volvo was chasing her down one path and the mad woodkiller was down the other. If only she could reach her granddaughter's house. Then she would be quiet safe. The sound of the volvo's engine revving became louder and louder. The woodpecker's cries were blood-curdling. There was only one thing left to do. She must find the mobile home and phone her mother.

Getting to know a reader

Please consult with the teacher before doing this task. It is important that you choose the child together and that no unusual pressure or demands are placed upon that child. The activity is intended to strengthen your understanding of what is happening when children read so that you can provide appropriate support.

Child: _____ **Date:** _____

Book: _____

Child's attitudes to reading

Child's attitudes to books

What does the child know already about books?
   Author
   Title
   Pages
   Front/back
   Left to right
   Top to bottom
   What is a word?
   What is a letter?
   Spaces
   Full stops

Words that caused problems on this occasion

Letters that caused a problem on this occasion

Strategies used to tackle unknown words

Use of contextual clues

Memory of story

Discussion of own experiences relating to story

Supporting reading across the curriculum

Consider the following situations in a nursery and jot down ideas for resources and types of adult intervention to support and develop aspects of a child's reading.

Situation	Resources	Intervention
Sand tray		
Water tray		
Home corner		
Role play office		
Writing corner		
Technology workshop		
Making displays		
Cooking		
Planting seeds		
Local walk		
Using plasticine		
Computer		

Handwriting

This task is designed to help you understand how a child feels when he or she is learning to write. Using the hand which you do not normally use for writing, make a copy of the text on the top half of the page by writing on the bottom half of the page. Make a note of how it feels and of any changes you needed to make in order to compensate.

Why did Mr Fish (an acquaintance of George Bernard Shaw) like to spell his name in a more interesting way?

Mr GHOTIUGH
GH = f as in tough
O= i as in women
TI= sh as in initial
UGH= silent as in though

YOUR COPY...

Reflecting on your own practices

During the course of one week, try to focus on two questions from the list below. Use the process to identify any areas in which you might like to seek further advice from the teacher. Make a list of action points on the back of a photocopy of this sheet.

- When a child asks you for a spelling what things can you do to encourage independence and confidence?

- When do you ask children to read their writing to you?

- How do you respond to the content of children's writing?

- How do you focus on the good elements before pointing out the mistakes?

- How do you point out mistakes and when is it necessary to limit the number of mistakes to be discussed with the child?

- How might you encourage the child to discuss other ideas of his or her own?

- How do you suggest new ideas to the child without taking over the ownership of the work?

- How do you show children that you value their contributions?

- If a child offers a totally wrong answer how do you respond so that he or she does not feel embarrassed or discouraged?

- How can you set mini-targets to help a child through a much larger task?

- When children are practising handwriting do you observe the strokes?

Recording children's knowledge of languages in addition to English

This activity is a mini-survey of children's knowledge of other languages in addition to English. Such a record was first pioneered in London using *The Primary Language Record* (ILEA 1988) and was found to be an invaluable way of gaining insight into the breadth of children's language knowledge.

In consultation with your teacher mentor and head teacher, or whoever is in charge of your workplace, choose eight children for the survey. If possible try to include children who you know are bilingual or multilingual. If you can talk to the children's parents as well as the children you will gain a much broader view of the language repertoire of your group.

Name:	Understands:	Speaks:	Reads:	Writes:

Bilingual group observations

Having received the approval of the person in charge, try to conduct a range of five-minute observations of bilingual children working in groups of different sizes, including pairs. It is advisable to use a fresh copy of this sheet for each situation you observe. The schedule below is designed to make your recording easier, but do go ahead and design a different format based on your own ideas if you wish.

Try to observe from a distance, otherwise you will be drawn into the activity! If it is possible and appropriate, a tape recorder could be placed close to the children as a back-up. In this case it is only fair to explain to the children that you are interested in their talk, but that you want them to ignore the taping. They will probably enjoy listening to the tape themselves afterwards.

As you observe, note down the type of talk for each child as it happens using the following codes : E = explaining, Q = questioning, A = answering, R = repeating, D = describing . At the end your entries might look like this:
CHILD A   EEEQAAAAAA
If they used their home language, place a circle round the letter.

ACTIVITY AREA:

RESOURCES:

HOME LANGUAGE: CHILD A   CHILD B
                     CHILD C   CHILD D
                     CHILD E   CHILD F

A

B

C

D

E

F

When your observations are complete, look at them carefully and note any patterns or differences between the different situations. Make a list of four points which you feel might influence your future practice as a result of conducting this exercise.

References

Bentley, D. *et al.* (1999) *The Catch Up Programme. Updated Edition.* See website: www.thecathupproject.org

Clay, M. M. (1975) *What Did I Write?* Auckland: Heinemann Educational Books.

Clipson-Boyles, S. B. (1996) *Early Years Writing Stages.* Oxford: Oxford Brookes University School of Education.

Cummins, J. (1994) 'The acquisition of English as a second language', in Sprangen-Urbschat, K. and Pritchard, R. (eds) *Kids Come in All Languages*, 36–62. New Delaware: International Reading Association.

Department for Education (1994) *The Code of Practice on the Idenfication and Assessment of Special Educational Needs.* London: HMSO.

Department for Education (1995) *English in the National Curriculum.* London: HMSO.

DfEE (1998) *The National Literacy Strategy Framework for Teaching.* London: DfEE.

DfEE (1999) *The National Literacy Strategy: Additional Literacy Support.* London: DfEE.

DfEE and QCA (1999a) *The National Curriculum for England. English.* London: QCA.

DfEE and QCA (1999b) *Early Learning Goals.* London: QCA.

DfEE and QCA (2000) *Curriculum Guidance for the Foundation Stage.* London: QCA.

Department of Education and Science (1988) *English for Ages 5–16* (The Cox Report). London: HMSO.

Department of Education and Science (1990) *Starting with Quality: Report of the Committee of Inquiry into the Educational Experiences Offered to Three- and Four-Year-Olds* (Rumbold Report). London: HMSO.

Department of Employment and Department of Education and Science (1986) *Working Together: Education and Training.* London: HMSO.

Francis, H. (1992) 'Patterns of reading development in the first school', *British Journal of Educational Psychology*, **62**(2), 225–23.

Gentry, J. R. (1987) *Spel. . . is a Four-Letter Word.* Leamington Spa: Scholastic.

ILEA (1988) *The Primary Language Record.* London: Centre for Language and Primary English.

Multilingual Resources for Children Project (1995) *Building Bridges: Multilingual Resources for Children.* Reading: Reading and Language Information Centre.

SCAA, TTA and ACAC (1996) *A Guide to the National Curriculum.* London: HMSO.

Siraj-Blatchford, I. (1992) 'Why understanding cultural differences is not enough', in Pugh, G. (ed.) *Contemporary Issues in the Early Years – Working Collaboratively for Children*, 104–21. London: NCB and Paul Chapman Publishing.

Smith, F. (1982) *Writing and the Writer.* Oxford: Heinemann.

Vygotsky, L. S. (1978) *Mind in Society: The Development of Higher Psychological Processes.* Cambridge, USA: Harvard University Press.

Wells, G. (1985) *Language, Learning and Education.* Windsort: NFER-Nelson.

Index